ArtScroll Mesorah Series®

מגילת אסתר

The Family megillah

THE BOOK OF ESTHER

Translation and marginal annotations
based on the ArtScroll Megillas Esther *by*
Rabbi Meir Zlotowitz

Introduction by
Rabbi Nosson Scherman

Designed and Produced by
Sheah Brander

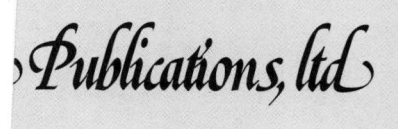
Publications, ltd

FIRST EDITION
Sixteen Impressions . . . December 1982 — January 2006

SECOND EDITION
First Impression . . . January 2007

Published and Distributed by
MESORAH PUBLICATIONS, Ltd.
4401 Second Avenue
Brooklyn, New York 11232

Distributed in Europe by
LEHMANNS
Unit E, Viking Business Park
Rolling Mill Road
Jarrow, Tyne & Wear NE32 3DP
England

Distributed in Australia & New Zealand by
GOLDS WORLD OF JUDAICA
3-13 William Street
Balaclava, Melbourne 3183
Victoria Australia

Distributed in Israel by
SIFRIATI / A. GITLER — BOOKS
6 Hayarkon Street
Bnei Brak 51127

Distributed in South Africa by
KOLLEL BOOKSHOP
Ivy Common 105 William Road
Norwood 2192, Johannesburg, South Africa

ISBN:
0-89906-192-3 (paperback)

Typography by CompuScribe at ArtScroll Studios, Ltd.
4401 Second Avenue / Brooklyn, N.Y. 11232 / (718) 921-9000

Printed in the United States of America

Esther — A Book for the Ages

One of the great Chassidic masters of the last century remarked that because the festival of Purim was proclaimed during a period of Jewish exile, it has special meaning whenever there is a diaspora (*Sfas Emes*). The Book of Esther tells a thrilling spellbinding story. What a pity that it is so familiar to many of us that it no longer thrills us as it should. At the very least, however, let us look at the ancient tale and see how much it speaks to our time, for our Sages saw in it the kind of lessons from which the nation should learn — or which it will be doomed to repeat.

The 20th century has given a new relevance not only to the genocidal intention of Haman, but to his method of pursuing it. No longer can anyone say — as some did a hundred years ago — that modern society could never produce, much less condone, a monster whose announced intention was "to destroy, to slay, and to exterminate all Jews, young and old, children and women, in a single day ..." (*Esther* 3:13). How naive it now seems that people seriously believed that mass extermination of human beings could never be contemplated by civilized people. Now we know that Haman was the first, but lamentably, surely not the last. Nor have we recovered from the Holocaust perpetrated by the modern Haman, who came six million souls closer to achieving his goal than did his ancient model.

How striking and ominously familiar were Haman's arguments to gain Ahasuerus' acquiescence. As given briefly in the Book of Esther (3:8-9) and amplified by the Talmudic Sages, Haman's diatribe has been echoed by anti-Semites throughout the ages: Jews are separatists, elitists, racists. They hold themselves apart from all other peoples of realm. They will not blend into our culture or religion. They are damaging to the unity of the kingdom. Why should the king tolerate their divisive presence — is it worth the price? Would not the world be better served if this nuisance, this friendless nation, were removed from our midst? And, finally, the state will derive an immense economic benefit from the disappearance of this pariah people.

So sophisticated a discourse to justify such a foul end! But it should not surprise anyone. Throughout our history we have been similarly maligned and our oppressors have indignantly insisted that they were forced to take heroic measures to defend themselves against little Israel. The laws of the Third Reich were carefully phrased in terms that deceived many a naive observer into believing that a tormented nation — call it Persia, Spain, Russia, Germany, or the United Nations — was merely seeking to protect itself from an internal cancer.

What ignited Haman's anger? There are two answers: the obvious one and the true one.

What ignited Haman's anger? There are two answers: the obvious one and the true one. The obvious one was Mordechai's obstinacy. Proud Jew that he was, Mordechai refused to bow to Haman, who, as tradition teaches, brazenly paraded with an image of his idol dangling from his neck. Mordechai insisted that there had to be at least one Jew who would not sacrifice dignity on the altar of expediency; would Haman love Israel any more if even Mordechai's knees scraped the ground in obeisance to a pagan deity? The infuriated Haman sought revenge in the annihilation not only of Mordechai but of his entire people. And the pundits of the time surely reveled in the charge that "stiff-necked" Mordechai was to blame for Israel's catastrophe.

The pundits of the time surely reveled in the charge that "stiff-necked" Mordechai was to blame for Israel's catastrophe.

But, as the Sages teach, that was not the *true* reason for the destruction that threatened Israel. Nine years earlier the Jews had ignored the warnings of Mordechai and his fellow sages not to indulge in forbidden foods and acts at the lavish feast of Ahasuerus. Let Jews be loyal to their government — yes; but let them not set aside their Torah to do so. The people wouldn't listen. They argued that Ahasuerus would never understand their abstinence. He would accuse them of disloyalty, of harboring secret hopes, and planning conspiracies to return to *Eretz Yisrael*. If their loyalties were to Jerusalem rather than Shushan, they would be branded traitors, and the punishment for treason is ...

If their loyalties were to Jerusalem rather than Shushan, they would be branded traitors,

Dare we antagonize a paranoid, insecure monarch like Ahasuerus? Dare we place our nation's survival at risk by antagonizing a king whose caprices are notorious? And when Ahasuerus ordered the execution of his beloved Queen Vashti simply because she refused to disgrace herself publicly to satisfy his whim — didn't that prove that we were wise and right not to provoke his mercurial anger?

On the Divine scales, however, Mordechai's judgment was right. Jews do not survive by committing spiritual suicide.

On the Divine scales, however, Mordechai's judgment was right. Jews do not survive by committing spiritual suicide. For if a Jew lacks pride in his Jewishness, by what virtue does he deserve the right to preserve his separate identity?

The nation had precipitated its own downfall by an act of cowardly faithlessness; only by a parallel act of communal courage could it save itself. Mordechai began the process by defying Haman's decree to bow. *His* knee would not bend. *He* would not grovel. Then came Esther's turn.

Unknown to King Ahasuerus or his viceroy Haman, Queen Esther was a Jewess, and Mordechai demanded that she intercede with the king. She hesitated. Logic dictated that she wait for a more opportune moment to plead with Ahasuerus (see 4:9-11). But Mordechai would not accept her argument. Could it be that she was somewhat complacent because *she* enjoyed the safety of anonymity and the security of the throne? After all, Ahasuerus had not the slightest suspicion that his beloved was a member of the race he had consigned to the pyre of history. Would she have been so "rational" if *she* had been in as much jeopardy as her brethren?

Could it be that she was somewhat complacent because she enjoyed the safety of anonymity and the security of the throne?

Mordechai replied harshly to Esther: "Do not imagine that you will be able to escape in the king's palace any more than the rest of the Jews. For if you persist in keeping silent at a time like this, relief and deliverance will come to the Jews from some other place, while you and your father's house will perish. And who knows whether it was just for such a time as this that you attained the royal position!" (4:13-14).

A new insight into communal responsibility: To help one's fellow Jews is a privilege, not a chore. The nation will always survive somehow, but the one who spurns its entreaties will himself be doomed. And furthermore, no matter how exalted someone's position or lavish his fortune, let him always regard it as but a means to serve the common good. Now Esther knew why she had been raised to the throne — to save her people, and if she failed to do so she might well be condemning *herself* to oblivion, while another path to salvation would surely open for them.

The nation will always survive somehow, but the one who spurns its entreaties will himself be doomed.

Esther was more than equal to the challenge, and her bravery, dedication, and cunning precipitated a swiftly moving series of events that brought new glory to her people, and that doomed Haman. But even this is not the primary lesson of Purim.

Amazingly, God's Name does not appear in the Megillah — and precisely that is its lesson: God's ways are not always obvious, His miracles are most often not illuminated by lightning nor punctuated by thunder. In the concisely written 167-verse Megillah, no seas split, no heavens roar, no dry bones come to life, but in the truest sense the greatest of all

God's Name does not appear in the Megillah — and precisely that is its lesson: God's ways are not always obvious.

miracles *is* narrated in the Purim story: It is the miracle of God's constant supervision and control of events.

With the period of Esther and Mordechai, a new emphasis was added to Jewish history. We had to find God's hand not in the splitting sea or heavenly fire, but in everyday events.

The story of the Megillah spanned nine years, and only at the very end did the pieces of God's jigsaw puzzle begin coming together. Suddenly widely separate links began to move together to form a chain and widely separated chains joined to become the anchor upon which Jewish survival was secured. And simple logic turned turned out to be wrong; Mordechai had been right all along in not participating in Ahasuerus' orgy and in not bowing to Haman.

One set of links: Ahasuerus' feast led to the execution of Vashti which led to the coronation of Esther. Because Esther was queen, she was in a position to approach the king to save her people and she could lull Haman into complacency by inviting him to her private banquet.

Another set of links: Bigthana and Teresh plotted to kill Ahasuerus. Because Esther had secured a royal appointment for Mordechai, he was positioned to overhear them and report the scheme to Esther. She told the king of Mordechai's loyalty. It was inscribed in the royal chronicle, there to lay forgotten until the fateful night when God disturbed the king's sleep.

A third set of links: The king promoted Haman and everyone was required to bow to him, but Mordechai refused. Assured of his power and influence — even with the queen! — Haman built a gallows and sought royal permission to hang Mordechai, just when Ahasuerus learned that it was Mordechai who had once saved his life.

When the appropriate climactic time arrived, the pieces of God's jigsaw puzzle came together and formed the destruction of Haman and most of Amalek, and salvation for the Jews.

The events of those ancient days determine the mode of Purim's annual observance. The Megillah is read morning and evening, and all Jews are required to hear it; its lesson is too important to be restricted only to those who normally attend the synagogue regularly. Even people who are unable to hear the public reading should arrange to have it read for them

from a ritually valid Megillah scroll. When we hear the Megillah, however, let us remember the eternal lesson beneath the rousing story.

The celebration of Purim is unique among Jewish festivals. Purim is celebrated with an excess of food, drink, and frivolity, because we are marking an event when our *physical* lives were threatened, unlike other festivals that commemorate primarily spiritual dangers and salvations.

Furthermore, Purim is a holiday of Jewish fellowship as well, because among the tools that forged the miracle were a sense of communal responsibility, a sense of concern for the plight of every Jew. So the requirements of the day include gifts to friends and to the poor. For indeed, we are one and we must take positive steps to remain one.

Purim shows us how to live and survive in a hostile environment where not only survival is in question but even God's Presence seems to be absent.

As *Sfas Emes* taught, Purim is indeed a festival aimed primarily at Jews without their Temple, for it shows us how to live and survive in a hostile environment where not only survival is in question but even God's Presence seems to be absent. Thanks to Purim, we feel more secure about survival and we can "see" God's hand even where He is invisible.

Rabbi Nosson Scherman

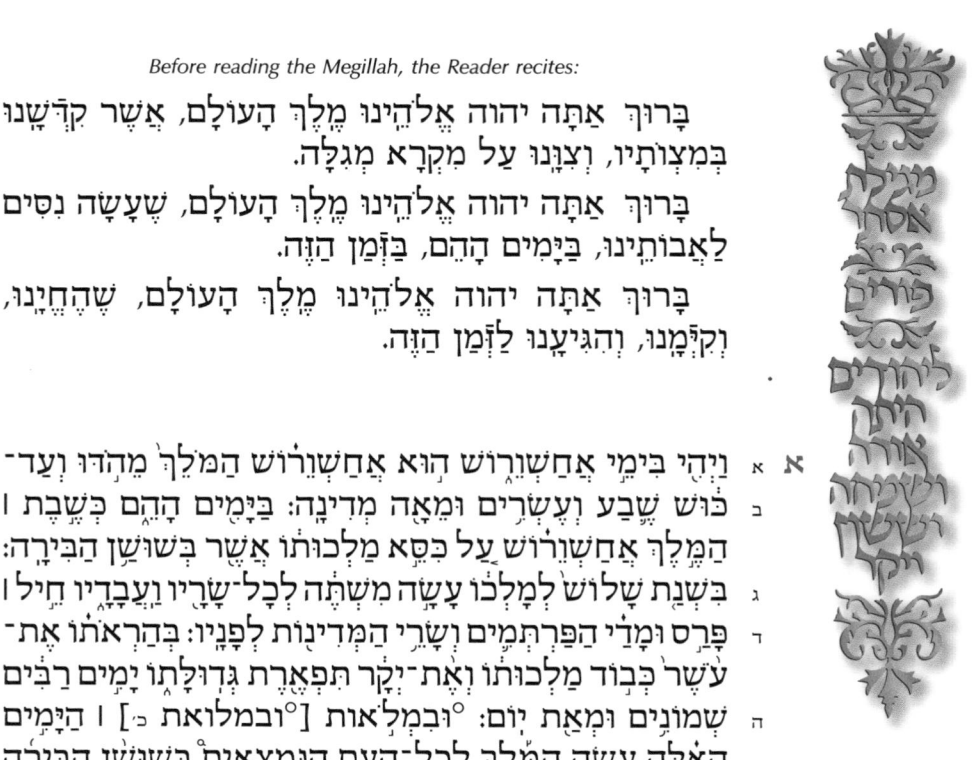

Before reading the Megillah, the Reader recites:

בָּרוּךְ אַתָּה יהוה אֱלֹהֵינוּ מֶלֶךְ הָעוֹלָם, אֲשֶׁר קִדְּשָׁנוּ
בְּמִצְוֹתָיו, וְצִוָּנוּ עַל מִקְרָא מְגִלָּה.

בָּרוּךְ אַתָּה יהוה אֱלֹהֵינוּ מֶלֶךְ הָעוֹלָם, שֶׁעָשָׂה נִסִּים
לַאֲבוֹתֵינוּ, בַּיָּמִים הָהֵם, בַּזְּמַן הַזֶּה.

בָּרוּךְ אַתָּה יהוה אֱלֹהֵינוּ מֶלֶךְ הָעוֹלָם, שֶׁהֶחֱיָנוּ,
וְקִיְּמָנוּ, וְהִגִּיעָנוּ לַזְּמַן הַזֶּה.

א

א וַיְהִי בִּימֵי אֲחַשְׁוֵרוֹשׁ הוּא אֲחַשְׁוֵרוֹשׁ הַמֹּלֵךְ מֵהֹדּוּ וְעַד־
ב כּוּשׁ שֶׁבַע וְעֶשְׂרִים וּמֵאָה מְדִינָה: בַּיָּמִים הָהֵם כְּשֶׁבֶת ׀
הַמֶּלֶךְ אֲחַשְׁוֵרוֹשׁ עַל כִּסֵּא מַלְכוּתוֹ אֲשֶׁר בְּשׁוּשַׁן הַבִּירָה:
ג בִּשְׁנַת שָׁלוֹשׁ לְמָלְכוֹ עָשָׂה מִשְׁתֶּה לְכָל־שָׂרָיו וַעֲבָדָיו חֵיל ׀
ד פָּרַס וּמָדַי הַפַּרְתְּמִים וְשָׂרֵי הַמְּדִינוֹת לְפָנָיו: בְּהַרְאֹתוֹ אֶת־
עֹשֶׁר כְּבוֹד מַלְכוּתוֹ וְאֶת־יְקָר תִּפְאֶרֶת גְּדוּלָּתוֹ יָמִים רַבִּים
ה שְׁמוֹנִים וּמְאַת יוֹם: °וּבִמְלֹאות [°וּבִמְלוֹאת כ] ׀ הַיָּמִים
הָאֵלֶּה עָשָׂה הַמֶּלֶךְ לְכָל־הָעָם הַנִּמְצְאִים בְּשׁוּשַׁן הַבִּירָה
לְמִגָּדוֹל וְעַד־קָטָן מִשְׁתֶּה שִׁבְעַת יָמִים בַּחֲצַר גִּנַּת בִּיתַן
ו הַמֶּלֶךְ: חוּר ׀ כַּרְפַּס וּתְכֵלֶת אָחוּז בְּחַבְלֵי־בוּץ וְאַרְגָּמָן
עַל־גְּלִילֵי כֶסֶף וְעַמּוּדֵי שֵׁשׁ מִטּוֹת ׀ זָהָב וָכֶסֶף עַל רִצְפַת
ז בַּהַט־וָשֵׁשׁ וְדַר וְסֹחָרֶת: וְהַשְׁקוֹת בִּכְלֵי זָהָב וְכֵלִים
ח מִכֵּלִים שׁוֹנִים וְיַיִן מַלְכוּת רָב כְּיַד הַמֶּלֶךְ: וְהַשְּׁתִיָּה כַדָּת
אֵין אֹנֵס כִּי־כֵן ׀ יִסַּד הַמֶּלֶךְ עַל כָּל־רַב בֵּיתוֹ לַעֲשׂוֹת
ט כִּרְצוֹן אִישׁ־וָאִישׁ: גַּם וַשְׁתִּי הַמַּלְכָּה עָשְׂתָה
י מִשְׁתֵּה נָשִׁים בֵּית הַמַּלְכוּת אֲשֶׁר לַמֶּלֶךְ אֲחַשְׁוֵרוֹשׁ: בַּיּוֹם
הַשְּׁבִיעִי כְּטוֹב לֵב־הַמֶּלֶךְ בַּיָּיִן אָמַר לִמְהוּמָן בִּזְּתָא
חַרְבוֹנָא בִּגְתָא וַאֲבַגְתָא זֵתַר וְכַרְכַּס שִׁבְעַת הַסָּרִיסִים
יא הַמְשָׁרְתִים אֶת־פְּנֵי הַמֶּלֶךְ אֲחַשְׁוֵרוֹשׁ: לְהָבִיא אֶת־וַשְׁתִּי
הַמַּלְכָּה לִפְנֵי הַמֶּלֶךְ בְּכֶתֶר מַלְכוּת לְהַרְאוֹת הָעַמִּים
יב וְהַשָּׂרִים אֶת־יָפְיָהּ כִּי־טוֹבַת מַרְאֶה הִיא: וַתְּמָאֵן הַמַּלְכָּה
וַשְׁתִּי לָבוֹא בִּדְבַר הַמֶּלֶךְ אֲשֶׁר בְּיַד הַסָּרִיסִים וַיִּקְצֹף
יג הַמֶּלֶךְ מְאֹד וַחֲמָתוֹ בָּעֲרָה בוֹ: וַיֹּאמֶר הַמֶּלֶךְ

Blessed are You, HASHEM, our God, King of the universe, Who has sanctified us with His commandments and has commanded us regarding the reading of the Megillah.

Blessed are You, HASHEM, our God, King of the universe, Who has wrought miracles for our forefathers, in those days at this season.

Blessed are You, HASHEM, our God, King of the universe, Who has kept us alive, sustained us and brought us to this season.

1 / 1. THE FEASTS OF AHASUERUS

— successor to Cyrus toward the end of the 70 years of the Babylonian exile [4th Century B.C.E.].

3. *In the third year:* 3395 from Creation.

According to his (erroneous) calculation, the 70th year of the Jews' exile had passed, thus belying the prophets who had foretold the exile's end after 70 years, and Ahasuerus rejoiced in this frustration of Jewish hope; he had completed the building of his magnificent throne; he was finally secure in his reign; he took Vashti as his queen. Thus the causes for such a lavish feast (*Midrash*).

6. The letter ח has the numerical value of 8. In the Megillah the ח of the word חור, *white garments*, is enlarged to imply that on that climactic day Ahasuerus adorned himself with the eight garments of the High Priest. In punishment for this, he suffered the multiple evils of the resulting episode with Vashti, her death, his embarrassment and subsequent depression (*Alkabetz*).

9. VASHTI REFUSES THE KING'S SUMMONS

Vashti was the daughter of Belshazzar, and granddaughter of Nebuchadnezzer.

11. *[Wearing] the royal crown.* She was to wear *only the royal crown,* i.e., unclothed (*Midrash*).

Vashti *refused,* not because of modesty. The reason for her refusal was that God caused leprosy to break out on her, and paved the way for her downfall (*Midrash*).

¹**A**nd it came to pass in the days of Ahasuerus — he is the Ahasuerus who reigned from Hodu to Cush, a hundred and twenty-seven provinces — ² in those days, when King Ahasuerus sat on his royal throne which was in Shushan the capital, ³ in the third year of his reign, he made a feast for all his officials and his servants; the army of Persia and Media; the nobles and officials of the provinces being present; ⁴ when he displayed the riches of his glorious kingdom and the honor of his splendrous majesty for many days, a hundred and eighty days. ⁵ And when these days were fulfilled, the king made a seven-day feast for all the people who were present in Shushan the capital, great and small alike, in the courtyard of the garden of the king's palace. ⁶ There were [hangings of] white, fine cotton, and turquoise wool, held with cords of fine linen and purple wool, upon silver rods and marble pillars; the couches of gold and silver were on a pavement of variegated marble. ⁷ The drinks were served in golden vessels — vessels of diverse form — and royal wine in abundance, in accordance with the king's wealth. ⁸ And the drinking was according to the law, there was no coercion, for so the king had established for every officer of his house to do according to each man's pleasure.

⁹ Vashti the queen also made a feast for the women in the royal house of King Ahasuerus. ¹⁰ On the seventh day, when the heart of the king was merry with wine, he told Mehuman, Bizzetha, Harbona, Bigtha and Abagtha, Zethar and Carcas, the seven chamberlains who attended King Ahasuerus, ¹¹ to bring Vashti the queen before the king [wearing] the royal crown, to show off to the people and the officials her beauty, for she was beautiful of appearance. ¹² But Queen Vashti refused to come at the king's command [conveyed] by the hand of the chamberlains; the king therefore became very enraged and his wrath burned in him.

לַחֲכָמִים יֹדְעֵי הָעִתִּים כִּי־כֵן דְּבַר הַמֶּלֶךְ לִפְנֵי כָּל־יֹדְעֵי
דָּת וָדִין: וְהַקָּרֹב אֵלָיו כַּרְשְׁנָא שֵׁתָר אַדְמָתָא תַרְשִׁישׁ מֶרֶס **יד**
מַרְסְנָא מְמוּכָן שִׁבְעַת שָׂרֵי ׀ פָּרַס וּמָדַי רֹאֵי פְּנֵי הַמֶּלֶךְ
הַיֹּשְׁבִים רִאשֹׁנָה בַּמַּלְכוּת: כְּדָת מַה־לַּעֲשׂוֹת בַּמַּלְכָּה **טו**
וַשְׁתִּי עַל ׀ אֲשֶׁר לֹא־עָשְׂתָה אֶת־מַאֲמַר הַמֶּלֶךְ אֲחַשְׁוֵרוֹשׁ
בְּיַד הַסָּרִיסִים: וַיֹּאמֶר °מְמוּכָן [°מוּמְכָן כ] **טז**
לִפְנֵי הַמֶּלֶךְ וְהַשָּׂרִים לֹא עַל־הַמֶּלֶךְ לְבַדּוֹ עָוְתָה וַשְׁתִּי
הַמַּלְכָּה כִּי עַל־כָּל־הַשָּׂרִים וְעַל־כָּל־הָעַמִּים אֲשֶׁר בְּכָל־
מְדִינוֹת הַמֶּלֶךְ אֲחַשְׁוֵרוֹשׁ: כִּי־יֵצֵא דְבַר־הַמַּלְכָּה עַל־ **יז**
כָּל־הַנָּשִׁים לְהַבְזוֹת בַּעְלֵיהֶן בְּעֵינֵיהֶן בְּאָמְרָם הַמֶּלֶךְ
אֲחַשְׁוֵרוֹשׁ אָמַר לְהָבִיא אֶת־וַשְׁתִּי הַמַּלְכָּה לְפָנָיו וְלֹא־
בָאָה: וְהַיּוֹם הַזֶּה תֹּאמַרְנָה ׀ שָׂרוֹת פָּרַס־וּמָדַי אֲשֶׁר **יח**
שָׁמְעוּ אֶת־דְּבַר הַמַּלְכָּה לְכֹל שָׂרֵי הַמֶּלֶךְ וּכְדַי בִּזָּיוֹן
וָקָצֶף: אִם־עַל־הַמֶּלֶךְ טוֹב יֵצֵא דְבַר־מַלְכוּת מִלְּפָנָיו **יט**
וְיִכָּתֵב בְּדָתֵי פָרַס־וּמָדַי וְלֹא יַעֲבוֹר אֲשֶׁר לֹא־תָבוֹא
וַשְׁתִּי לִפְנֵי הַמֶּלֶךְ אֲחַשְׁוֵרוֹשׁ וּמַלְכוּתָהּ יִתֵּן הַמֶּלֶךְ
לִרְעוּתָהּ הַטּוֹבָה מִמֶּנָּה: וְנִשְׁמַע פִּתְגָם הַמֶּלֶךְ אֲשֶׁר־ **כ**
יַעֲשֶׂה בְּכָל־מַלְכוּתוֹ כִּי רַבָּה הִיא וְכָל־הַנָּשִׁים יִתְּנוּ יְקָר
לְבַעְלֵיהֶן לְמִגָּדוֹל וְעַד־קָטָן: וַיִּיטַב הַדָּבָר בְּעֵינֵי הַמֶּלֶךְ **כא**
וְהַשָּׂרִים וַיַּעַשׂ הַמֶּלֶךְ כִּדְבַר מְמוּכָן: וַיִּשְׁלַח סְפָרִים אֶל־ **כב**
כָּל־מְדִינוֹת הַמֶּלֶךְ אֶל־מְדִינָה וּמְדִינָה כִּכְתָבָהּ וְאֶל־עַם
וָעַם כִּלְשׁוֹנוֹ לִהְיוֹת כָּל־אִישׁ שֹׂרֵר בְּבֵיתוֹ וּמְדַבֵּר כִּלְשׁוֹן
עַמּוֹ: **ב** **א** אַחַר הַדְּבָרִים הָאֵלֶּה כְּשֹׁךְ חֲמַת הַמֶּלֶךְ

אֲחַשְׁוֵרוֹשׁ זָכַר אֶת־וַשְׁתִּי וְאֵת אֲשֶׁר־עָשָׂתָה וְאֵת אֲשֶׁר
נִגְזַר עָלֶיהָ: וַיֹּאמְרוּ נַעֲרֵי־הַמֶּלֶךְ מְשָׁרְתָיו יְבַקְשׁוּ לַמֶּלֶךְ **ב**
נְעָרוֹת בְּתוּלוֹת טוֹבוֹת מַרְאֶה: וְיַפְקֵד הַמֶּלֶךְ פְּקִידִים **ג**
בְּכָל־מְדִינוֹת מַלְכוּתוֹ וְיִקְבְּצוּ אֶת־כָּל־נַעֲרָה־בְתוּלָה
טוֹבַת מַרְאֶה אֶל־שׁוּשַׁן הַבִּירָה אֶל־בֵּית הַנָּשִׁים אֶל־יַד
הֵגֶא סְרִיס הַמֶּלֶךְ שֹׁמֵר הַנָּשִׁים וְנָתוֹן תַּמְרֻקֵיהֶן: וְהַנַּעֲרָה **ד**
אֲשֶׁר תִּיטַב בְּעֵינֵי הַמֶּלֶךְ תִּמְלֹךְ תַּחַת וַשְׁתִּי וַיִּיטַב הַדָּבָר
בְּעֵינֵי הַמֶּלֶךְ וַיַּעַשׂ כֵּן: **אִישׁ יְהוּדִי הָיָה בְּשׁוּשַׁן** **ה**
הַבִּירָה וּשְׁמוֹ מָרְדֳּכַי בֶּן יָאִיר בֶּן־שִׁמְעִי בֶּן־קִישׁ אִישׁ
יְמִינִי: אֲשֶׁר הָגְלָה מִירוּשָׁלַיִם עִם־הַגֹּלָה אֲשֶׁר הָגְלְתָה **ו**

13. THE KING SEEKS ADVICE

13 Then the king spoke to the wise men, those who knew the times (for such was the king's procedure [to turn] to all who knew law and judgment), 14 those closest to him — Carshena, Shethar, Admatha, Tarshish, Meres, Marsena and Memucan, the seven officers of Persia and Media, who had access to the king, who sat first in the kingdom: 15 "By the law, what should be done to Queen Vashti for not having obeyed the bidding of the King Ahasuerus [conveyed] by the hand of the chamberlains?"

16. MEMUCHAN'S SUGGESTION

"Memuchan is Haman. Why was he called Memuchan? Because he was destined [מוכן] for destruction" (Talmud).

16 Memucan declared before the king and the officials, "Not only against the king has Vashti the queen done wrong, but against all the officials and all the people in all the provinces of King Ahasuerus. 17 For the queen's deed will go forth to all women, making their husbands contemptible in their eyes, when they will say, 'King Ahasuerus said to bring Vashti the queen before him, but she did not come!' 18 And this day the princesses of Persia and Media who have heard of the queen's deed will speak of it to all the king's officials, and there will be much contempt and rage. 19 If it pleases the king, let there go forth a royal edict from him, and let it be written into the laws of Persia and Media, that it not be revoked, that Vashti never again appear before King Ahasuerus; and let the king confer her royal estate upon another who is better than she. 20 Then, the king's decree which he will proclaim shall be heard throughout all his kingdom — great though it be — and all the wives will show respect to their husbands, great and

21. VASHTI IS DEPOSED

This proposal was favorable in the eyes of the king. "He gave the order and they brought in her head on a platter" (Midrash).

small alike." 21 This proposal was favorable in the eyes of the king and the officials, and the king did according to the word of Memucan; 22 and he sent letters into all the king's provinces, to each province in its own script, and to each people in its own language, [to the effect that] every man should rule in his own home, and speak the language of his own people.

2 / 1. AHASUERUS SEEKS A NEW QUEEN

He remembered the order he had given her to appear unclothed before him and how she refused, and how he had been wroth with her and put her to death (Midrash).

1After these things, when the wrath of King Ahasuerus subsided, he remembered Vashti, and what she had done, and what had been decreed against her. 2 Then the king's attendants said, "Let there be sought for the king young maidens of beautiful appearance; 3 and let the king appoint commissioners in all the provinces of his kingdom, that they gather together every young maiden of beautiful appearance to Shushan the capital, to the harem, under the charge of Hegai the king's chamberlain, guardian of the women; and let their cosmetics be given them. 4 Then, let the girl who pleases the king reign in place of Vashti." The matter pleased the king, and he did so.

5. MORDECHAI AND ESTHER

This verse is among the four verses said aloud in the synagogue by the congregation during the public reading of the Megillah.

5 **There was a Jewish man in Shushan the capital whose name was Mordechai son of Jair son of Shimei son of Kish, a Benjamite,** 6 who had been exiled from Jerusalem along with the exiles who had been exiled

עִם־יְכָנְיָה מֶֽלֶךְ־יְהוּדָה אֲשֶׁר הֶגְלָה נְבֽוּכַדְנֶאצַּר מֶֽלֶךְ בָּבֶֽל:

ז וַיְהִי אֹמֵן אֶת־הֲדַסָּה הִיא אֶסְתֵּר בַּת־דֹּדוֹ כִּי אֵין לָהּ אָב וָאֵם וְהַנַּעֲרָה יְפַת־תֹּֽאַר וְטוֹבַת מַרְאֶה וּבְמוֹת אָבִֽיהָ וְאִמָּהּ לְקָחָהּ מָרְדֳּכַי לוֹ לְבַֽת:

ח וַיְהִי בְּהִשָּׁמַע דְּבַר־הַמֶּֽלֶךְ וְדָתוֹ וּֽבְהִקָּבֵץ נְעָרוֹת רַבּוֹת אֶל־שׁוּשַׁן הַבִּירָה אֶל־יַד הֵגָי וַתִּלָּקַח אֶסְתֵּר אֶל־בֵּית הַמֶּֽלֶךְ אֶל־יַד הֵגַי שֹׁמֵר הַנָּשִֽׁים:

ט וַתִּיטַב הַנַּעֲרָה בְעֵינָיו וַתִּשָּׂא חֶֽסֶד לְפָנָיו וַיְבַהֵל אֶת־תַּמְרוּקֶֽיהָ וְאֶת־מָנוֹתֶֽהָ לָתֵת לָהּ וְאֵת שֶֽׁבַע הַנְּעָרוֹת הָרְאֻיוֹת לָֽתֶת־לָהּ מִבֵּית הַמֶּֽלֶךְ וַיְשַׁנֶּֽהָ וְאֶת־נַעֲרוֹתֶֽיהָ לְטוֹב בֵּית הַנָּשִֽׁים:

י לֹא־הִגִּידָה אֶסְתֵּר אֶת־עַמָּהּ וְאֶת־מֽוֹלַדְתָּהּ כִּי מָרְדֳּכַי צִוָּה עָלֶֽיהָ אֲשֶׁר לֹא־תַגִּֽיד:

יא וּבְכָל־יוֹם וָיוֹם מָרְדֳּכַי מִתְהַלֵּךְ לִפְנֵי חֲצַר בֵּית־הַנָּשִׁים לָדַֽעַת אֶת־שְׁלוֹם אֶסְתֵּר וּמַה־יֵּעָשֶׂה בָּֽהּ:

יב וּבְהַגִּיעַ תֹּר נַעֲרָה וְנַעֲרָה לָבוֹא ׀ אֶל־הַמֶּֽלֶךְ אֲחַשְׁוֵרוֹשׁ מִקֵּץ הֱיוֹת לָהּ כְּדָת הַנָּשִׁים שְׁנֵים עָשָׂר חֹֽדֶשׁ כִּי כֵּן יִמְלְאוּ יְמֵי מְרוּקֵיהֶן שִׁשָּׁה חֳדָשִׁים בְּשֶׁמֶן הַמֹּר וְשִׁשָּׁה חֳדָשִׁים בַּבְּשָׂמִים וּבְתַמְרוּקֵי הַנָּשִֽׁים:

יג וּבָזֶה הַֽנַּעֲרָה בָּאָה אֶל־הַמֶּֽלֶךְ אֵת כָּל־אֲשֶׁר תֹּאמַר יִנָּֽתֵן לָהּ לָבוֹא עִמָּהּ מִבֵּית הַנָּשִׁים עַד־בֵּית הַמֶּֽלֶךְ:

יד בָּעֶֽרֶב ׀ הִיא בָאָה וּבַבֹּֽקֶר הִיא שָׁבָה אֶל־בֵּית הַנָּשִׁים שֵׁנִי אֶל־יַד שַֽׁעַשְׁגַז סְרִיס הַמֶּֽלֶךְ שֹׁמֵר הַפִּֽילַגְשִׁים לֹא־תָבוֹא עוֹד אֶל־הַמֶּֽלֶךְ כִּי אִם־חָפֵץ בָּהּ הַמֶּֽלֶךְ וְנִקְרְאָה בְשֵֽׁם:

טו וּבְהַגִּיעַ תֹּר־אֶסְתֵּר בַּת־אֲבִיחַֽיִל ׀ דֹּד מָרְדֳּכַי אֲשֶׁר לָקַֽח־לוֹ לְבַת לָבוֹא אֶל־הַמֶּֽלֶךְ לֹא בִקְשָׁה דָּבָר כִּי אִם אֶת־אֲשֶׁר יֹאמַר הֵגַי סְרִיס־הַמֶּֽלֶךְ שֹׁמֵר הַנָּשִׁים וַתְּהִי אֶסְתֵּר נֹשֵׂאת חֵן בְּעֵינֵי כָּל־רֹאֶֽיהָ:

טז וַתִּלָּקַח אֶסְתֵּר אֶל־הַמֶּֽלֶךְ אֲחַשְׁוֵרוֹשׁ אֶל־בֵּית מַלְכוּתוֹ בַּחֹֽדֶשׁ הָעֲשִׂירִי הוּא־חֹֽדֶשׁ טֵבֵת בִּשְׁנַת־שֶֽׁבַע לְמַלְכוּתֽוֹ:

יז וַיֶּאֱהַב הַמֶּֽלֶךְ אֶת־אֶסְתֵּר מִכָּל־הַנָּשִׁים וַתִּשָּׂא־חֵן וָחֶֽסֶד לְפָנָיו מִכָּל־הַבְּתוּלוֹת וַיָּֽשֶׂם כֶּֽתֶר־מַלְכוּת בְּרֹאשָׁהּ וַיַּמְלִיכֶֽהָ תַּֽחַת וַשְׁתִּֽי:

יח וַיַּעַשׂ הַמֶּֽלֶךְ מִשְׁתֶּה גָדוֹל לְכָל־שָׂרָיו וַעֲבָדָיו אֵת מִשְׁתֵּה אֶסְתֵּר וַהֲנָחָה לַמְּדִינוֹת עָשָׂה וַיִּתֵּן מַשְׂאֵת כְּיַד הַמֶּֽלֶךְ:

יט-כ וּבְהִקָּבֵץ בְּתוּלוֹת שֵׁנִית וּמָרְדֳּכַי יֹשֵׁב בְּשַֽׁעַר־הַמֶּֽלֶךְ: אֵין אֶסְתֵּר מַגֶּֽדֶת מֽוֹלַדְתָּהּ וְאֶת־עַמָּהּ כַּאֲשֶׁר צִוָּה עָלֶֽיהָ

8. ESTHER IS BROUGHT TO THE HAREM

14. Having consorted with the king, it would not be proper for them to marry other men. They were required to return to the harem and remain there for the rest of their lives as concubines, to await the possibility of being crowned queen if the king found no one better.

17. ESTHER IS CHOSEN QUEEN

19. THE SECOND GATHERING

with Jeconiah king of Judah, whom Nebuchadnezzar king of Babylon had exiled. ⁷ And he had reared Hadassah, she is Esther, his uncle's daughter; for she had neither father nor mother. The maiden was finely featured and beautiful of appearance, and when her father and mother had died, Mordechai adopted her as [his] daughter. ⁸ So it came to pass, when the king's bidding and decree were announced, and when many young maidens were being brought together to Shushan the capital, under the charge of Hegai, that Esther was taken to the king's palace, under the charge of Hegai, guardian of the women. ⁹ The girl was pleasing in his eyes, and she found favor before him; he hurriedly prepared her cosmetics and her allowance of delicacies to present [to] her, along with the seven attendants from the king's palace, and he transferred her and her maidens to the best [quarters] in the harem. ¹⁰ Esther had not told of her people or her kindred, for Mordechai had instructed her not to tell. ¹¹ Day after day Mordechai would walk about in front of the courtyard of the harem to learn about Esther's well-being and what would become of her.

¹² Now when each maiden's turn arrived to come to King Ahasuerus, after having been treated according to the law prescribed for women for twelve months (for so was the prescribed length of their anointing accomplished: six months with oil of myrrh, and six months with perfumes and feminine cosmetics) — ¹³ and when the girl came in this manner to the king, she was given whatever she requested to accompany her from the harem to the king's palace. ¹⁴ In the evening she would come, and in the morning she would return to the second harem in the charge of Shaashgaz, the king's chamberlain, guardian of the concubines. She would never again come to the king unless the king desired her, and she was summoned by name.

¹⁵ Now when the turn came for Esther daughter of Abihail uncle of Mordechai (who had adopted her as [his] daughter) to come to the king, she requested nothing except that which Hegai, the king's chamberlain, guardian of the women, had advised. Esther would find favor in the eyes of all who saw her. ¹⁶ Esther was taken to King Ahasuerus into his royal palace in the tenth month, which is the month of Teves, in the seventh year of his reign. ¹⁷ The king loved Esther more than all the women, and she found more favor and kindness before him than all the other maidens; so that he set the royal crown upon her head, and made her queen in place of Vashti. ¹⁸ Then the king made a great banquet for all his officers and his servants — it was Esther's banquet — and he proclaimed an amnesty for the provinces, and gave gifts worthy of the king's hand.

¹⁹ And when the maidens were gathered together the second time, and Mordechai sat at the king's gate, ²⁰ Esther still told nothing of her kindred or her people as Mordechai had instructed her; for Esther continued to obey

מָרְדֳּכָי וְאֶת־מַאֲמַר מָרְדֳּכַי אֶסְתֵּר עֹשָׂה כַּאֲשֶׁר הָיְתָה

בְאׇמְנָה אִתּֽוֹ: בַּיָּמִים הָהֵם וּמׇרְדֳּכַי יֹשֵׁב

כא בְּשַֽׁעַר־הַמֶּלֶךְ קָצַף בִּגְתָן וָתֶרֶשׁ שְׁנֵֽי־סָרִיסֵי הַמֶּלֶךְ

מִשֹּׁמְרֵי הַסַּף וַיְבַקְשׁוּ לִשְׁלֹחַ יָד בַּמֶּלֶךְ אֲחַשְׁוֵרֹֽשׁ:

כב וַיִּוָּדַע הַדָּבָר לְמׇרְדֳּכַי וַיַּגֵּד לְאֶסְתֵּר הַמַּלְכָּה וַתֹּאמֶר

כג אֶסְתֵּר לַמֶּלֶךְ בְּשֵׁם מׇרְדֳּכָֽי: וַיְבֻקַּשׁ הַדָּבָר וַיִּמָּצֵא וַיִּתָּלוּ

שְׁנֵיהֶם עַל־עֵץ וַיִּכָּתֵב בְּסֵפֶר דִּבְרֵי הַיָּמִים לִפְנֵי

הַמֶּֽלֶךְ: ג א אַחַר ׀ הַדְּבָרִים הָאֵלֶּה גִּדַּל הַמֶּלֶךְ

אֲחַשְׁוֵרוֹשׁ אֶת־הָמָן בֶּן־הַמְּדָתָא הָאֲגָגִי וַֽיְנַשְּׂאֵהוּ וַיָּשֶׂם

ב אֶת־כִּסְאוֹ מֵעַל כׇּל־הַשָּׂרִים אֲשֶׁר אִתּֽוֹ: וְכׇל־עַבְדֵי הַמֶּלֶךְ

אֲשֶׁר־בְּשַֽׁעַר הַמֶּלֶךְ כֹּרְעִים וּמִֽשְׁתַּחֲוִים לְהָמָן כִּי־כֵן צִוָּה־

ג לוֹ הַמֶּלֶךְ וּמׇרְדֳּכַי לֹא יִכְרַע וְלֹא יִֽשְׁתַּחֲוֶֽה: וַיֹּאמְרוּ עַבְדֵי

הַמֶּלֶךְ אֲשֶׁר־בְּשַֽׁעַר הַמֶּלֶךְ לְמׇרְדֳּכָי מַדּוּעַ אַתָּה עוֹבֵר

ד אֵת מִצְוַת הַמֶּֽלֶךְ: וַיְהִי °כְּאׇמְרָם [°בְּאׇמְרָם כ] אֵלָיו יוֹם

וָיוֹם וְלֹא שָׁמַע אֲלֵיהֶם וַיַּגִּידוּ לְהָמָן לִרְאוֹת הֲיַעַמְדוּ דִּבְרֵי

ה מׇרְדֳּכַי כִּֽי־הִגִּיד לָהֶם אֲשֶׁר־הוּא יְהוּדִֽי: וַיַּרְא הָמָן כִּי־אֵין

ו מׇרְדֳּכַי כֹּרֵעַ וּמִֽשְׁתַּחֲוֶה לוֹ וַיִּמָּלֵא הָמָן חֵמָֽה: וַיִּבֶז בְּעֵינָיו

לִשְׁלֹחַ יָד בְּמׇרְדֳּכַי לְבַדּוֹ כִּֽי־הִגִּידוּ לוֹ אֶת־עַם מׇרְדֳּכָי

וַיְבַקֵּשׁ הָמָן לְהַשְׁמִיד אֶת־כׇּל־הַיְּהוּדִים אֲשֶׁר בְּכׇל־מַלְכוּת

ז אֲחַשְׁוֵרוֹשׁ עַם מׇרְדֳּכָֽי: בַּחֹדֶשׁ הָרִאשׁוֹן הוּא־חֹדֶשׁ נִיסָן

בִּשְׁנַת שְׁתֵּים עֶשְׂרֵה לַמֶּלֶךְ אֲחַשְׁוֵרוֹשׁ הִפִּיל פּוּר הוּא

הַגּוֹרָל לִפְנֵי הָמָן מִיּוֹם ׀ לְיוֹם וּמֵחֹדֶשׁ לְחֹדֶשׁ שְׁנֵים־עָשָׂר

ח הוּא־חֹדֶשׁ אֲדָֽר: וַיֹּאמֶר הָמָן לַמֶּלֶךְ

אֲחַשְׁוֵרוֹשׁ יֶשְׁנוֹ עַם־אֶחָד מְפֻזָּר וּמְפֹרָד בֵּין הָעַמִּים בְּכֹל

מְדִינוֹת מַלְכוּתֶךָ וְדָתֵיהֶם שֹׁנוֹת מִכׇּל־עָם וְאֶת־דָּתֵי

ט הַמֶּלֶךְ אֵינָם עֹשִׂים וְלַמֶּלֶךְ אֵֽין־שֹׁוֶה לְהַנִּיחָֽם: אִם־עַל־

הַמֶּלֶךְ טוֹב יִכָּתֵב לְאַבְּדָם וַעֲשֶׂרֶת אֲלָפִים כִּכַּר־כֶּסֶף

אֶשְׁקוֹל עַל־יְדֵי עֹשֵׂי הַמְּלָאכָה לְהָבִיא אֶל־גִּנְזֵי הַמֶּֽלֶךְ:

י וַיָּסַר הַמֶּלֶךְ אֶת־טַבַּעְתּוֹ מֵעַל יָדוֹ וַֽיִּתְּנָהּ לְהָמָן בֶּן־

יא הַמְּדָתָא הָאֲגָגִי צֹרֵר הַיְּהוּדִֽים: וַיֹּאמֶר הַמֶּלֶךְ לְהָמָן

הַכֶּסֶף נָתוּן לָךְ וְהָעָם לַעֲשׂוֹת בּוֹ כַּטּוֹב בְּעֵינֶֽיךָ: וַיִּקָּרְאוּ

יב סֹפְרֵי הַמֶּלֶךְ בַּחֹדֶשׁ הָרִאשׁוֹן בִּשְׁלוֹשָׁה עָשָׂר יוֹם בּוֹ

וַיִּכָּתֵב כְּֽכׇל־אֲשֶׁר־צִוָּה הָמָן אֶל אֲחַשְׁדַּרְפְּנֵי־הַמֶּלֶךְ וְאֶל־

21. MORDECHAI FOILS A PLOT AGAINST THE KING

Being a member of the Sanhedrin Mordechai knew 70 languages. They spoke in their native Tarsian tongue in Mordechai's presence, not expecting him to understand them (*Talmud*).

[21] In those days, while Mordechai was sitting at the king's gate, Bigthan and Teresh, two of the king's chamberlains of the guardians of the threshold, became enraged and sought to send [their] hand against King Ahasuerus. [22] The matter became known to Mordechai, who told it to Esther the queen, and Esther informed the king in Mordechai's name. [23] The matter was investigated and found [to be true], and they were both hanged on a gallows. It was recorded in the book of chronicles in the king's presence.

3 / 1. HAMAN IS ADVANCED

Haman was a descendant of Agag, king of Amalek [*I Samuel* 15:9].

2. To make it manifest that the homage due him was of an idolatrous character, Haman had the image of an idol fastened to his clothes, so that whoever bowed down before him worshiped an idol at the same time. Therefore Mordechai would not bow down or prostrate himself (*Midrash*).

[1] **A**fter these things King Ahasuerus promoted Haman son of Hammedatha the Agagite and elevated him; he set his seat above all the officers who were with him. [2] All the king's servants at the king's gate would bow down and prostrate themselves before Haman, for so had the king commanded concerning him. But Mordechai would not bow and would not prostrate himself. [3] So the king's servants who were at the king's gate said to Mordechai, "Why do you disobey the king's command?" [4] Now it happened when they said this to him day after day and he did not heed them, they told Haman, to see whether Mordechai's words would prevail; for he had told them that he was a Jew. [5] When Haman, himself, saw that Mordechai did not bow down and prostrate himself before him, Haman was filled with wrath. [6] However, it seemed contemptible to him to send [his] hand against Mordechai alone, for they had told him of the people of Mordechai. So Haman sought to destroy all the Jews who were throughout the entire kingdom of Ahasuerus — the people of Mordechai. [7] In the first month, which is the month of Nissan, in the twelfth year of King Ahasuerus, pur (that is, the lot) was cast in the presence of Haman from day to day, and from month to month, to the twelfth month, which is the month of Adar.

6. HAMAN PLANS THE DESTRUCTION OF ALL THE JEWS

The reaction of Haman to a personal affront is typical of the most rabid anti-Semites throughout the ages.

8. HAMAN SLANDERS THE JEWS TO THE KING

Haman said: "They eat and drink and despise the throne. For if a fly falls into a Jew's cup, he throws out the fly and drinks the wine; but if His Majesty were to merely touch his cup, he would throw it to the ground and not drink from it" (*Talmud*).

9. The price Haman was ready to pay for the right to exterminate the Jews, 10,000 talents, was 24 million ounces, or 750 tons of silver!

10. THE KING CONSENTS TO THE DESTRUCTION OF THE JEWS

[8] Then Haman said to King Ahasuerus, "There is a certain people scattered abroad and dispersed among the peoples in all the provinces of your realm. Their laws are different from every other people's and they do not observe the king's laws; therefore it is not befitting the king to tolerate them. [9] If it pleases the king, let it be recorded that they be destroyed; and I will pay ten thousand silver talents into the hands of those who perform the duties, for deposit in the king's treasuries." [10] So the king removed his signet ring from his hand, and gave it to Haman son of Hammedatha the Agagite, enemy of the Jews. [11] Then the king said to Haman, "The silver is given to you, the people also, to do with as you see fit." [12] The king's scribes were summoned on the thirteenth day of the first month, and everything was written exactly as Haman had dictated, to the king's satraps, to the

הַפַּחוֹת אֲשֶׁר ׀ עַל־מְדִינָה וּמְדִינָה וְאֶל־שָׂרֵי עַם וָעָם
מְדִינָה וּמְדִינָה כִּכְתָבָהּ וְעַם וָעָם כִּלְשׁוֹנוֹ בְּשֵׁם הַמֶּלֶךְ
אֲחַשְׁוֵרֹשׁ נִכְתָּב וְנֶחְתָּם בְּטַבַּעַת הַמֶּלֶךְ: וְנִשְׁלוֹחַ סְפָרִים
יג בְּיַד הָרָצִים אֶל־כָּל־מְדִינוֹת הַמֶּלֶךְ לְהַשְׁמִיד לַהֲרֹג
וּלְאַבֵּד אֶת־כָּל־הַיְּהוּדִים מִנַּעַר וְעַד־זָקֵן טַף וְנָשִׁים בְּיוֹם
אֶחָד בִּשְׁלוֹשָׁה עָשָׂר לְחֹדֶשׁ שְׁנֵים־עָשָׂר הוּא־חֹדֶשׁ אֲדָר
וּשְׁלָלָם לָבוֹז: פַּתְשֶׁגֶן הַכְּתָב לְהִנָּתֵן דָּת בְּכָל־מְדִינָה
יד וּמְדִינָה גָּלוּי לְכָל־הָעַמִּים לִהְיוֹת עֲתִדִים לַיּוֹם הַזֶּה:
הָרָצִים יָצְאוּ דְחוּפִים בִּדְבַר הַמֶּלֶךְ וְהַדָּת נִתְּנָה
טו בְּשׁוּשַׁן הַבִּירָה וְהַמֶּלֶךְ וְהָמָן יָשְׁבוּ לִשְׁתּוֹת וְהָעִיר שׁוּשָׁן
נָבוֹכָה: ד א וּמָרְדֳּכַי יָדַע אֶת־כָּל־אֲשֶׁר נַעֲשָׂה
וַיִּקְרַע מָרְדֳּכַי אֶת־בְּגָדָיו וַיִּלְבַּשׁ שַׂק וָאֵפֶר וַיֵּצֵא בְּתוֹךְ
ב הָעִיר וַיִּזְעַק זְעָקָה גְדוֹלָה וּמָרָה: וַיָּבוֹא עַד לִפְנֵי שַׁעַר־
ג הַמֶּלֶךְ כִּי אֵין לָבוֹא אֶל־שַׁעַר הַמֶּלֶךְ בִּלְבוּשׁ שָׂק: וּבְכָל־
מְדִינָה וּמְדִינָה מְקוֹם אֲשֶׁר דְּבַר־הַמֶּלֶךְ וְדָתוֹ מַגִּיעַ אֵבֶל
גָּדוֹל לַיְּהוּדִים וְצוֹם וּבְכִי וּמִסְפֵּד שַׂק וָאֵפֶר יֻצַּע לָרַבִּים:
ד °וַתָּבוֹאֶנָה [וַתָּבוֹאֶינָה כ] נַעֲרוֹת אֶסְתֵּר וְסָרִיסֶיהָ וַיַּגִּידוּ
לָהּ וַתִּתְחַלְחַל הַמַּלְכָּה מְאֹד וַתִּשְׁלַח בְּגָדִים לְהַלְבִּישׁ
ה אֶת־מָרְדֳּכַי וּלְהָסִיר שַׂקּוֹ מֵעָלָיו וְלֹא קִבֵּל: וַתִּקְרָא אֶסְתֵּר
לַהֲתָךְ מִסָּרִיסֵי הַמֶּלֶךְ אֲשֶׁר הֶעֱמִיד לְפָנֶיהָ וַתְּצַוֵּהוּ עַל־
ו מָרְדֳּכָי לָדַעַת מַה־זֶּה וְעַל־מַה־זֶּה: וַיֵּצֵא הֲתָךְ אֶל־מָרְדֳּכָי
ז אֶל־רְחוֹב הָעִיר אֲשֶׁר לִפְנֵי שַׁעַר־הַמֶּלֶךְ: וַיַּגֶּד־לוֹ מָרְדֳּכַי
אֵת כָּל־אֲשֶׁר קָרָהוּ וְאֵת ׀ פָּרָשַׁת הַכֶּסֶף אֲשֶׁר אָמַר הָמָן
לִשְׁקוֹל עַל־גִּנְזֵי הַמֶּלֶךְ °בַּיְּהוּדִים [בַּיְּהוּדִיִּים כ] לְאַבְּדָם:
ח וְאֶת־פַּתְשֶׁגֶן כְּתָב־הַדָּת אֲשֶׁר־נִתַּן בְּשׁוּשָׁן לְהַשְׁמִידָם נָתַן
לוֹ לְהַרְאוֹת אֶת־אֶסְתֵּר וּלְהַגִּיד לָהּ וּלְצַוּוֹת עָלֶיהָ לָבוֹא
ט אֶל־הַמֶּלֶךְ לְהִתְחַנֶּן־לוֹ וּלְבַקֵּשׁ מִלְּפָנָיו עַל־עַמָּהּ: וַיָּבוֹא
י הֲתָךְ וַיַּגֵּד לְאֶסְתֵּר אֵת דִּבְרֵי מָרְדֳּכָי: וַתֹּאמֶר אֶסְתֵּר לַהֲתָךְ
יא וַתְּצַוֵּהוּ אֶל־מָרְדֳּכָי: כָּל־עַבְדֵי הַמֶּלֶךְ וְעַם מְדִינוֹת הַמֶּלֶךְ
יֹדְעִים אֲשֶׁר כָּל־אִישׁ וְאִשָּׁה אֲשֶׁר יָבוֹא־אֶל־הַמֶּלֶךְ אֶל־
הֶחָצֵר הַפְּנִימִית אֲשֶׁר לֹא־יִקָּרֵא אַחַת דָּתוֹ לְהָמִית לְבַד
מֵאֲשֶׁר יוֹשִׁיט־לוֹ הַמֶּלֶךְ אֶת־שַׁרְבִיט הַזָּהָב וְחָיָה וַאֲנִי
יב לֹא נִקְרֵאתִי לָבוֹא אֶל־הַמֶּלֶךְ זֶה שְׁלוֹשִׁים יוֹם: וַיַּגִּידוּ

governors who were over every province, and to the officials of every people; [to] each province in its own script, and [to] each people in its own language; it was written in the name of King Ahasuerus, and it was sealed with the king's signet ring. [13] Letters were sent by courier to all the provinces of the king, to destroy, to slay and to exterminate all the Jews, from young to old, children and women, in one day, on the thirteenth of the twelfth month, which is the month of Adar, and to plunder their possessions. [14] Copies of the document were to be promulgated in every province, and be published to all peoples, for them to be prepared for that day. [15] The couriers went forth hurriedly by order of the king, and the edict was distributed in Shushan the capital. The king and Haman sat down to drink, but the city of Shushan was bewildered.

4 / 1. MORDECHAI AND THE JEWS MOURN

[1] Mordechai learned of all that had been done; and Mordechai tore his clothes and donned sackcloth and ashes. He went out into the midst of the city, and cried a loud and bitter cry. [2] He came until the front of the king's gate for it was forbidden to enter the king's gate in a garment of sackcloth. [3] And in every province, any place the king's command and his decree extended, there was great mourning among the Jews, and fasting and weeping and lament; sackcloth and ashes were spread out for the masses.

[4] And Esther's maidens came, as well as her chamberlains, and told her about it, and the queen was greatly distressed; she sent garments to clothe Mordechai, and to remove his sackcloth from upon him, but he would not accept [them].

[5] Then Esther summoned Hathach, one of the king's chamberlains whom he had stationed before her, and ordered him [to go] to Mordechai, to learn what this was about and why. [6] So Hathach went out to Mordechai to the city square, which was in front of the king's gate. [7] And Mordechai told him of all that had happened to him, and all about the sum of money that Haman had promised to pay to the royal treasuries for the annihilation of the Jews. [8] He also gave him a copy of the text of the decree that was distributed in Shushan for their destruction, so that he might show it to Esther and inform her, and bid her to go to the king, to implore of him, and to plead with him for her people.

[9] Hathach came and told Esther the words of Mordechai. [10] Then Esther told Hathach, and ordered him [to return] to Mordechai, [saying]: [11] "All the king's servants and the people of the king's provinces know that any man or woman who approaches the king in the inner court, who is not summoned, his law is one — to be put to death; except for the one to whom the king shall extend the gold scepter so that he may live. Now I, I have not been summoned to come to the king for these [past] thirty days."

8. MORDECHAI ASKS ESTHER TO INTERCEDE

10. ESTHER'S RECALCITRANT RESPONSE

לְמָרְדֳּכַי אֵת דִּבְרֵי אֶסְתֵּר: וַיֹּאמֶר מָרְדֳּכַי לְהָשִׁיב אֶל־ יג
אֶסְתֵּר אַל־תְּדַמִּי בְנַפְשֵׁךְ לְהִמָּלֵט בֵּית־הַמֶּלֶךְ מִכׇּל־
הַיְּהוּדִים: כִּי אִם־הַחֲרֵשׁ תַּחֲרִישִׁי בָּעֵת הַזֹּאת רֶוַח יד
וְהַצָּלָה יַעֲמוֹד לַיְּהוּדִים מִמָּקוֹם אַחֵר וְאַתְּ וּבֵית־אָבִיךְ
תֹּאבֵדוּ וּמִי יוֹדֵעַ אִם־לְעֵת כָּזֹאת הִגַּעַתְּ לַמַּלְכוּת:
וַתֹּאמֶר אֶסְתֵּר לְהָשִׁיב אֶל־מָרְדֳּכָי: לֵךְ כְּנוֹס אֶת־כׇּל־ טו-טז
הַיְּהוּדִים הַנִּמְצְאִים בְּשׁוּשָׁן וְצוּמוּ עָלַי וְאַל־תֹּאכְלוּ וְאַל־
תִּשְׁתּוּ שְׁלֹשֶׁת יָמִים לַיְלָה וָיוֹם גַּם־אֲנִי וְנַעֲרֹתַי אָצוּם כֵּן
וּבְכֵן אָבוֹא אֶל־הַמֶּלֶךְ אֲשֶׁר לֹא־כַדָּת וְכַאֲשֶׁר אָבַדְתִּי
אָבָדְתִּי: וַיַּעֲבֹר מׇרְדֳּכָי וַיַּעַשׂ כְּכֹל אֲשֶׁר־צִוְּתָה עָלָיו יז
אֶסְתֵּר: וַיְהִי | בַּיּוֹם הַשְּׁלִישִׁי וַתִּלְבַּשׁ אֶסְתֵּר מַלְכוּת ה א
וַתַּעֲמֹד בַּחֲצַר בֵּית־הַמֶּלֶךְ הַפְּנִימִית נֹכַח בֵּית הַמֶּלֶךְ
וְהַמֶּלֶךְ יוֹשֵׁב עַל־כִּסֵּא מַלְכוּתוֹ בְּבֵית הַמַּלְכוּת נֹכַח פֶּתַח
הַבָּיִת: וַיְהִי כִרְאוֹת הַמֶּלֶךְ אֶת־אֶסְתֵּר הַמַּלְכָּה עֹמֶדֶת ב
בֶּחָצֵר נָשְׂאָה חֵן בְּעֵינָיו וַיּוֹשֶׁט הַמֶּלֶךְ לְאֶסְתֵּר אֶת־
שַׁרְבִיט הַזָּהָב אֲשֶׁר בְּיָדוֹ וַתִּקְרַב אֶסְתֵּר וַתִּגַּע בְּרֹאשׁ
הַשַּׁרְבִיט: וַיֹּאמֶר לָהּ הַמֶּלֶךְ מַה־לָּךְ אֶסְתֵּר הַמַּלְכָּה וּמַה־ ג
בַּקָּשָׁתֵךְ עַד־חֲצִי הַמַּלְכוּת וְיִנָּתֵן לָךְ: וַתֹּאמֶר אֶסְתֵּר אִם־ ד
עַל־הַמֶּלֶךְ טוֹב יָבוֹא הַמֶּלֶךְ וְהָמָן הַיּוֹם אֶל־הַמִּשְׁתֶּה
אֲשֶׁר־עָשִׂיתִי לוֹ: וַיֹּאמֶר הַמֶּלֶךְ מַהֲרוּ אֶת־הָמָן לַעֲשׂוֹת ה
אֶת־דְּבַר אֶסְתֵּר וַיָּבֹא הַמֶּלֶךְ וְהָמָן אֶל־הַמִּשְׁתֶּה אֲשֶׁר־
עָשְׂתָה אֶסְתֵּר: וַיֹּאמֶר הַמֶּלֶךְ לְאֶסְתֵּר בְּמִשְׁתֵּה הַיַּיִן מַה־ ו
שְּׁאֵלָתֵךְ וְיִנָּתֵן לָךְ וּמַה־בַּקָּשָׁתֵךְ עַד־חֲצִי הַמַּלְכוּת
וְתֵעָשׂ: וַתַּעַן אֶסְתֵּר וַתֹּאמַר שְׁאֵלָתִי וּבַקָּשָׁתִי: אִם־ ז-ח
מָצָאתִי חֵן בְּעֵינֵי הַמֶּלֶךְ וְאִם־עַל־הַמֶּלֶךְ טוֹב לָתֵת אֶת־
שְׁאֵלָתִי וְלַעֲשׂוֹת אֶת־בַּקָּשָׁתִי יָבוֹא הַמֶּלֶךְ וְהָמָן אֶל־
הַמִּשְׁתֶּה אֲשֶׁר אֶעֱשֶׂה לָהֶם וּמָחָר אֶעֱשֶׂה כִּדְבַר הַמֶּלֶךְ:
וַיֵּצֵא הָמָן בַּיּוֹם הַהוּא שָׂמֵחַ וְטוֹב לֵב וְכִרְאוֹת הָמָן אֶת־ ט
מׇרְדֳּכַי בְּשַׁעַר הַמֶּלֶךְ וְלֹא־קָם וְלֹא־זָע מִמֶּנּוּ וַיִּמָּלֵא הָמָן
עַל־מׇרְדֳּכַי חֵמָה: וַיִּתְאַפַּק הָמָן וַיָּבוֹא אֶל־בֵּיתוֹ וַיִּשְׁלַח י
וַיָּבֵא אֶת־אֹהֲבָיו וְאֶת־זֶרֶשׁ אִשְׁתּוֹ: וַיְסַפֵּר לָהֶם הָמָן אֶת־ יא
כְּבוֹד עׇשְׁרוֹ וְרֹב בָּנָיו וְאֵת כׇּל־אֲשֶׁר גִּדְּלוֹ הַמֶּלֶךְ וְאֵת
אֲשֶׁר נִשְּׂאוֹ עַל־הַשָּׂרִים וְעַבְדֵי הַמֶּלֶךְ: וַיֹּאמֶר הָמָן אַף־ יב

13. MORDECHAI ENCOURAGES ESTHER

"You may, by some remote twist of fate, manage to save your body. But how will you save your soul?"

15. ESTHER AGREES TO GO UNSUMMONED TO THE KING

16. Esther limited the assembly to the Jews in Shushan because it would have been impossible to assemble Jews living further away on such short notice (*Gaon of Vilna*).

5 / 1. ESTHER GOES BEFORE THE KING

The third day — of the fast. It was, according to the Talmud, the first day of Passover.

4. ESTHER LAYS A TRAP FOR HAMAN

The first Hebrew letters of the words יָבֹא הַמֶּלֶךְ וְהָמָן הַיּוֹם form the Holy Name of God. This is one of the several places throughout the Megillah where God's Name is indirectly hinted (*Kad HaKemach*).

6. THE FIRST BANQUET

8. Esther's ruse worked. When Haman arrived at Esther's first banquet, he was apprehensive of Esther's reason for inviting him. He suspected a connection between the new edict concerning the Jews and his invitation. Only now, having left the first party at which he was overwhelmed with flattery, was he joyous and confident. He was unprepared, therefore, for the consequences of Esther's next banquet (*Alkabetz*).

[12] They related Esther's words to Mordechai. [13] Then Mordechai said to reply to Esther, "Do not imagine in your soul that you will be able to escape in the king's palace any more than the rest of the Jews. [14] For if you persist in keeping silent at a time like this, relief and deliverance will come to the Jews from another place, while you and your father's house will perish. And who knows whether it was just for such a time as this that you attained the royal position!'"

[15] Then Esther said to reply to Mordechai: [16] "Go, assemble all the Jews that are to be found in Shushan, and fast for me; do not eat or drink for three days, night or day: And I, with my maids, will fast also. Thus I will come to the king though it is unlawful; and if I perish, I perish." [17] Mordechai then left and did exactly as Esther had commanded him.

[1] **N**ow it came to pass on the third day, Esther donned royalty and stood in the inner courtyard of the king's palace facing the king's palace, while the king was sitting on his royal throne in the royal palace facing the entrance of the palace. [2] When the king noticed Esther the queen standing in the courtyard, she found favor in his eyes. The king extended to Esther the gold scepter that was in his hand, and Esther approached and touched the tip of the scepter.

[3] The king said to her, "What is it for you, O Esther the queen? And what is your petition? [Even if it be] until half the kingdom, it shall be granted you." [4] Esther said, "If it please the king, let the king and Haman come today to the banquet that I have prepared for him." [5] Then the king commanded, "Hasten Haman to fulfill Esther's word." So the king and Haman came to the banquet that Esther had prepared.

[6] The king said to Esther during the wine feast, "What is your request? It shall be granted you. And what is your petition? [Even if it be] until half the kingdom, it shall be fulfilled." [7] So Esther responded and said, "My request and my petition: [8] If I have found favor in the king's eyes, and if it pleases the king to grant my request and to fulfill my petition, let the king and Haman come to the banquet that I shall prepare for them, and tomorrow I shall fulfill the king's word."

[9] That day Haman went out joyful and exuberant. But when Haman noticed Mordechai in the king's gate and that he did not stand up and did not stir before him, Haman was filled with wrath at Mordechai. [10] [Nevertheless,] Haman restrained himself and went home. He sent and summoned his friends and his wife, Zeresh. [11] Haman recounted to them the glory of his wealth and of his many sons, and all [the ways] in which the king had promoted him and elevated him above the officials and royal servants. [12] Haman said, "Moreover, Esther the queen brought no one but myself to accompany the king to the banquet that she had prepared,

לֹא־הֵבִ֩יאָה֩ אֶסְתֵּ֨ר הַמַּלְכָּ֜ה עִם־הַמֶּ֤לֶךְ אֶל־הַמִּשְׁתֶּ֨ה
אֲשֶׁר־עָשָׂ֗תָה כִּ֣י אִם־אוֹתִ֑י וְגַם־לְמָחָ֛ר אֲנִ֥י קָרֽוּא־לָ֖הּ עִם־

יג הַמֶּֽלֶךְ: וְכָל־זֶ֕ה אֵינֶ֥נּוּ שֹׁוֶ֖ה לִ֑י בְּכָל־עֵ֗ת אֲשֶׁ֨ר אֲנִ֤י רֹאֶה֙
יד אֶת־מָרְדֳּכַ֣י הַיְּהוּדִ֔י יוֹשֵׁ֖ב בְּשַׁ֥עַר הַמֶּֽלֶךְ: וַתֹּ֣אמֶר לוֹ֩
זֶ֨רֶשׁ אִשְׁתּ֜וֹ וְכָל־אֹֽהֲבָ֗יו יַֽעֲשׂוּ־עֵץ֮ גָּבֹ֣הַּ חֲמִשִּׁ֣ים אַמָּה֒
וּבַבֹּ֣קֶר | אֱמֹ֣ר לַמֶּ֗לֶךְ וְיִתְל֤וּ אֶֽת־מָרְדֳּכַי֙ עָלָ֔יו וּבֹֽא־עִם־
הַמֶּ֥לֶךְ אֶל־הַמִּשְׁתֶּ֖ה שָׂמֵ֑חַ וַיִּיטַ֧ב הַדָּבָ֛ר לִפְנֵ֥י הָמָ֖ן וַיַּ֥עַשׂ
א הָעֵֽץ: בַּלַּ֣יְלָה הַה֔וּא נָֽדְדָ֖ה שְׁנַ֣ת הַמֶּ֑לֶךְ
וַיֹּ֗אמֶר לְהָבִ֞יא אֶת־סֵ֤פֶר הַזִּכְרֹנוֹת֙ דִּבְרֵ֣י הַיָּמִ֔ים וַיִּֽהְי֥וּ
ב נִקְרָאִ֖ים לִפְנֵ֥י הַמֶּֽלֶךְ: וַיִּמָּצֵ֣א כָת֗וּב אֲשֶׁר֩ הִגִּ֨יד מָרְדֳּכַ֜י
עַל־בִּגְתָ֣נָא וָתֶ֗רֶשׁ שְׁנֵי֙ סָֽרִיסֵ֣י הַמֶּ֔לֶךְ מִשֹּֽׁמְרֵ֖י הַסַּ֑ף אֲשֶׁ֧ר
ג בִּקְשׁוּ֙ לִשְׁלֹ֣חַ יָ֔ד בַּמֶּ֖לֶךְ אֲחַשְׁוֵֽרוֹשׁ: וַיֹּ֣אמֶר הַמֶּ֔לֶךְ מַֽה־
נַּֽעֲשָׂ֞ה יְקָ֧ר וּגְדוּלָ֛ה לְמָרְדֳּכַ֖י עַל־זֶ֑ה וַיֹּ֨אמְר֜וּ נַֽעֲרֵ֤י הַמֶּ֨לֶךְ֙
ד מְשָׁ֣רְתָ֔יו לֹֽא־נַֽעֲשָׂ֥ה עִמּ֖וֹ דָּבָֽר: וַיֹּ֥אמֶר הַמֶּ֖לֶךְ מִ֣י בֶֽחָצֵ֑ר
וְהָמָ֣ן בָּ֗א לַֽחֲצַ֤ר בֵּית־הַמֶּ֨לֶךְ֙ הַחִ֣יצוֹנָ֔ה לֵאמֹ֣ר לַמֶּ֔לֶךְ
ה לִתְלוֹת֙ אֶֽת־מָרְדֳּכַ֔י עַל־הָעֵ֖ץ אֲשֶׁר־הֵכִ֥ין לֽוֹ: וַיֹּ֨אמְר֜וּ
נַֽעֲרֵ֤י הַמֶּ֨לֶךְ֙ אֵלָ֔יו הִנֵּ֧ה הָמָ֛ן עֹמֵ֥ד בֶּֽחָצֵ֖ר וַיֹּ֥אמֶר הַמֶּ֖לֶךְ
ו יָבֽוֹא: וַיָּבוֹא֮ הָמָן֒ וַיֹּ֤אמֶר לוֹ֙ הַמֶּ֔לֶךְ מַֽה־לַּֽעֲשׂ֔וֹת בָּאִ֕ישׁ
אֲשֶׁ֥ר הַמֶּ֖לֶךְ חָפֵ֣ץ בִּֽיקָר֑וֹ וַיֹּ֤אמֶר הָמָן֙ בְּלִבּ֔וֹ לְמִ֞י יַחְפֹּ֥ץ
ז הַמֶּ֛לֶךְ לַֽעֲשׂ֥וֹת יְקָ֖ר יוֹתֵ֥ר מִמֶּֽנִּי: וַיֹּ֥אמֶר הָמָ֖ן אֶל־הַמֶּ֑לֶךְ
ח אִ֕ישׁ אֲשֶׁ֥ר הַמֶּ֖לֶךְ חָפֵ֣ץ בִּֽיקָר֑וֹ יָבִ֨יאוּ֙ לְב֣וּשׁ מַלְכ֔וּת אֲשֶׁ֥ר
לָֽבַשׁ־בּ֖וֹ הַמֶּ֑לֶךְ וְס֗וּס אֲשֶׁ֨ר רָכַ֤ב עָלָיו֙ הַמֶּ֔לֶךְ וַֽאֲשֶׁ֥ר נִתַּ֛ן
ט כֶּ֥תֶר מַלְכ֖וּת בְּרֹאשֽׁוֹ: וְנָת֨וֹן הַלְּב֜וּשׁ וְהַסּ֗וּס עַל־יַד־אִ֞ישׁ
מִשָּׂרֵ֤י הַמֶּ֨לֶךְ֙ הַֽפַּרְתְּמִ֔ים וְהִלְבִּ֨ישׁוּ֙ אֶת־הָאִ֔ישׁ אֲשֶׁ֥ר הַמֶּ֖לֶךְ
חָפֵ֣ץ בִּֽיקָר֑וֹ וְהִרְכִּיבֻ֤הוּ עַל־הַסּוּס֙ בִּרְח֣וֹב הָעִ֔יר וְקָֽרְא֣וּ
י לְפָנָ֔יו כָּ֚כָה יֵֽעָשֶׂ֣ה לָאִ֔ישׁ אֲשֶׁ֥ר הַמֶּ֖לֶךְ חָפֵ֥ץ בִּֽיקָרֽוֹ: וַיֹּ֨אמֶר
הַמֶּ֜לֶךְ לְהָמָ֗ן מַהֵ֞ר קַ֤ח אֶת־הַלְּבוּשׁ֙ וְאֶת־הַסּוּס֙ כַּֽאֲשֶׁ֣ר
דִּבַּ֔רְתָּ וַֽעֲשֵׂה־כֵן֙ לְמָרְדֳּכַ֣י הַיְּהוּדִ֔י הַיּוֹשֵׁ֖ב בְּשַׁ֣עַר הַמֶּ֑לֶךְ
יא אַל־תַּפֵּ֣ל דָּבָ֔ר מִכֹּ֖ל אֲשֶׁ֥ר דִּבַּֽרְתָּ: וַיִּקַּ֤ח הָמָן֙ אֶת־הַלְּב֣וּשׁ
וְאֶת־הַסּ֔וּס וַיַּלְבֵּ֖שׁ אֶֽת־מָרְדֳּכָ֑י וַיַּרְכִּיבֵ֨הוּ֙ בִּרְח֣וֹב הָעִ֔יר
וַיִּקְרָ֣א לְפָנָ֔יו כָּ֚כָה יֵֽעָשֶׂ֣ה לָאִ֔ישׁ אֲשֶׁ֥ר הַמֶּ֖לֶךְ חָפֵ֥ץ בִּֽיקָרֽוֹ:
יב וַיָּ֥שָׁב מָרְדֳּכַ֖י אֶל־שַׁ֣עַר הַמֶּ֑לֶךְ וְהָמָן֙ נִדְחַ֣ף אֶל־בֵּית֔וֹ אָבֵ֖ל
יג וַֽחֲפ֥וּי רֹֽאשׁ: וַיְסַפֵּ֨ר הָמָ֜ן לְזֶ֤רֶשׁ אִשְׁתּוֹ֙ וּלְכָל־אֹ֣הֲבָ֔יו אֵ֖ת

13. Notice that Haman did not mention to his wife and children that he was angry because of Mordechai's refusal to bow down to him; he thought it beneath his dignity to admit that such a minor slight could ruffle him so. Rather he claimed that he was angry because *"Mordechai the Jew was sitting at the king's gate"* and he was totally unworthy of such a high honor (*Me'am Loez*).

and tomorrow, too, I am invited by her along with the king. [13] Yet all this is worth nothing to me so long as I see Mordechai the Jew sitting at the king's gate." [14] So his wife, Zeresh, as well as all his friends, said to him, "Let them make a gallows, fifty cubits high; and in the morning speak to the king and have them hang Mordechai on it. Then, accompany the king to the banquet in good spirits." This suggestion pleased Haman, and he had the gallows made.

6 / 1. MORDECHAI IS FINALLY REWARDED

[1] That night the king's sleep was disturbed so he commanded to bring the book of records, the chronicles, and that they be read before the king. [2] And it was found written [there] that Mordechai had denounced Bigthana and Teresh, two of the king's chamberlains of the guardians of the threshold, who had sought to send [their] hand against King Ahasuerus. [3] The king said, "What honor or majesty has been done for Mordechai for this?" The king's attendants, his ministrants, said, "Nothing has been done for him." [4] The king said, "Who is in the courtyard?" (Now Haman was [just] coming into the outer courtyard of the royal palace to speak to the king about hanging Mordechai on the gallows that he had prepared for him.) [5] So the king's attendants said to him, "Behold! Haman stands in the courtyard." And the king said, "Let him enter." [6] Haman entered and the king said to him, "What should be done for the man whom the king desires to honor?" Now Haman said in his heart, *Whom would the king especially want to honor more than me?* [7] So Haman said to the king, "For the man whom the king desires to honor, [8] have them bring royal attire that the king has worn and a horse upon which the king has ridden, one with a royal crown placed on his head. [9] Then let the attire and the horse be given over into the hand of one of the king's most noble officials, and let them dress the man whom the king desires to honor, and have him ride on the horse through the city square, and let them proclaim before him, 'This is what shall be done for the

10. HAMAN'S HUMILIATION

man whom the king desires to honor.' " [10] Then the king said to Haman, "Hurry, take the attire and the horse as you have said, and do all this for Mordechai the Jew, who sits at the king's gate. Do not omit a single detail of all that you have suggested!" [11] So Haman took the garment and the horse and dressed Mordechai, and had him ride through the city square, and proclaimed before him, "This is what shall be done for the man whom the king desires to honor."

13. HAMAN'S DOOM IS FORECAST

[12] Mordechai returned to the king's gate; but Haman hurried home, despondent and with his head covered. [13] Haman told his wife, Zeresh, and all his friends everything

כָּל־אֲשֶׁ֣ר קָרָ֑הוּ וַיֹּ֩אמְרוּ֩ ל֨וֹ חֲכָמָ֜יו וְזֶ֣רֶשׁ אִשְׁתּ֗וֹ אִ֣ם מִזֶּ֣רַע
הַיְּהוּדִ֡ים מׇרְדֳּכַ֞י אֲשֶׁר֩ הַחִלּ֨וֹתָ לִנְפֹּ֤ל לְפָנָיו֙ לֹא־תוּכַ֣ל ל֔וֹ
כִּֽי־נָפ֥וֹל תִּפּ֖וֹל לְפָנָֽיו: עוֹדָם֙ מְדַבְּרִ֣ים עִמּ֔וֹ וְסָרִיסֵ֥י הַמֶּ֖לֶךְ

ז א הִגִּ֑יעוּ וַיַּבְהִ֙לוּ֙ לְהָבִ֣יא אֶת־הָמָ֔ן אֶל־הַמִּשְׁתֶּ֖ה אֲשֶׁר־
עָשְׂתָ֥ה אֶסְתֵּֽר: וַיָּבֹ֧א הַמֶּ֛לֶךְ וְהָמָ֖ן לִשְׁתּ֥וֹת עִם־אֶסְתֵּ֖ר
ב הַמַּלְכָּֽה: וַיֹּ֩אמֶר֩ הַמֶּ֨לֶךְ לְאֶסְתֵּ֜ר גַּ֣ם בַּיּ֤וֹם הַשֵּׁנִי֙ בְּמִשְׁתֵּ֣ה
הַיַּ֔יִן מַה־שְּׁאֵלָתֵ֛ךְ אֶסְתֵּ֥ר הַמַּלְכָּ֖ה וְתִנָּ֣תֵֽן לָ֑ךְ וּמַה־
ג בַּקָּשָׁתֵ֛ךְ עַד־חֲצִ֥י הַמַּלְכ֖וּת וְתֵעָֽשׂ: וַתַּ֨עַן אֶסְתֵּ֤ר הַמַּלְכָּה֙
וַתֹּאמַ֔ר אִם־מָצָ֨אתִי חֵ֤ן בְּעֵינֶ֙יךָ֙ הַמֶּ֔לֶךְ וְאִם־עַל־הַמֶּ֖לֶךְ
ד ט֑וֹב תִּנָּֽתֶן־לִ֤י נַפְשִׁי֙ בִּשְׁאֵ֣לָתִ֔י וְעַמִּ֖י בְּבַקָּשָׁתִֽי: כִּ֤י נִמְכַּ֙רְנוּ֙
אֲנִ֣י וְעַמִּ֔י לְהַשְׁמִ֖יד לַהֲר֣וֹג וּלְאַבֵּ֑ד וְ֠אִלּ֠וּ לַעֲבָדִ֨ים
וְלִשְׁפָח֤וֹת נִמְכַּ֙רְנוּ֙ הֶחֱרַ֔שְׁתִּי כִּ֣י אֵ֥ין הַצָּ֛ר שֹׁוֶ֖ה בְּנֵ֥זֶק
ה הַמֶּֽלֶךְ: וַיֹּ֙אמֶר֙ הַמֶּ֣לֶךְ אֲחַשְׁוֵר֔וֹשׁ וַיֹּ֖אמֶר
לְאֶסְתֵּ֣ר הַמַּלְכָּ֑ה מִ֣י ה֥וּא זֶ֛ה וְאֵֽי־זֶ֥ה ה֖וּא אֲשֶׁר־מְלָא֥וֹ לִבּ֖וֹ
ו לַעֲשׂ֥וֹת כֵּֽן: וַתֹּ֣אמֶר אֶסְתֵּ֔ר אִ֚ישׁ צַ֣ר וְאוֹיֵ֔ב הָמָ֥ן הָרָ֖ע הַזֶּ֑ה
ז וְהָמָ֣ן נִבְעַ֔ת מִלִּפְנֵ֥י הַמֶּ֖לֶךְ וְהַמַּלְכָּֽה: וְהַמֶּ֜לֶךְ קָ֤ם בַּחֲמָתוֹ֙
מִמִּשְׁתֵּ֣ה הַיַּ֔יִן אֶל־גִּנַּ֖ת הַבִּיתָ֑ן וְהָמָ֣ן עָמַ֗ד לְבַקֵּ֤שׁ עַל־נַפְשׁוֹ֙
מֵֽאֶסְתֵּ֣ר הַמַּלְכָּ֔ה כִּ֣י רָאָ֔ה כִּֽי־כָלְתָ֥ה אֵלָ֛יו הָרָעָ֖ה מֵאֵ֥ת
ח הַמֶּֽלֶךְ: וְהַמֶּ֡לֶךְ שָׁב֩ מִגִּנַּ֨ת הַבִּיתָ֜ן אֶל־בֵּ֣ית ׀ מִשְׁתֵּ֣ה
הַיַּ֗יִן וְהָמָן֙ נֹפֵ֔ל עַל־הַמִּטָּה֙ אֲשֶׁ֣ר אֶסְתֵּ֣ר עָלֶ֔יהָ וַיֹּ֣אמֶר
הַמֶּ֗לֶךְ הֲ֠גַ֠ם לִכְבּ֧וֹשׁ אֶת־הַמַּלְכָּ֛ה עִמִּ֖י בַּבָּ֑יִת הַדָּבָ֗ר יָצָא֙
ט מִפִּ֣י הַמֶּ֔לֶךְ וּפְנֵ֥י הָמָ֖ן חָפֽוּ: וַיֹּ֣אמֶר חַ֠רְבוֹנָ֠ה אֶחָ֨ד מִן־
הַסָּרִיסִ֜ים לִפְנֵ֣י הַמֶּ֗לֶךְ גַּ֣ם הִנֵּֽה־הָעֵ֡ץ אֲשֶׁר־עָשָׂ֨ה הָמָ֜ן
לְֽמׇרְדֳּכַ֗י אֲשֶׁ֨ר דִּבֶּר־ט֣וֹב עַל־הַמֶּ֔לֶךְ עֹמֵ֖ד בְּבֵ֣ית הָמָ֑ן
י גָּבֹ֖הַּ חֲמִשִּׁ֣ים אַמָּ֑ה וַיֹּ֥אמֶר הַמֶּ֖לֶךְ תְּלֻ֥הוּ עָלָֽיו: וַיִּתְלוּ֙
אֶת־הָמָ֔ן עַל־הָעֵ֖ץ אֲשֶׁר־הֵכִ֣ין לְמׇרְדֳּכָ֑י וַחֲמַ֥ת הַמֶּ֖לֶךְ
ח א שָׁכָֽכָה: בַּיּ֣וֹם הַה֗וּא נָתַ֞ן הַמֶּ֤לֶךְ
אֲחַשְׁוֵרוֹשׁ֙ לְאֶסְתֵּ֣ר הַמַּלְכָּ֔ה אֶת־בֵּ֥ית הָמָ֖ן צֹרֵ֣ר °הַיְּהוּדִ֑ים
[°הַיְּהוּדִיִּים כ׳] וּמׇרְדֳּכַ֗י בָּ֚א לִפְנֵ֣י הַמֶּ֔לֶךְ כִּֽי־הִגִּ֥ידָה אֶסְתֵּ֖ר
ב מַ֥ה הֽוּא־לָֽהּ: וַיָּ֨סַר הַמֶּ֜לֶךְ אֶת־טַבַּעְתּ֗וֹ אֲשֶׁ֤ר הֶֽעֱבִיר֙
מֵֽהָמָ֔ן וַֽיִּתְּנָ֖הּ לְמׇרְדֳּכָ֑י וַתָּ֧שֶׂם אֶסְתֵּ֛ר אֶת־מׇרְדֳּכַ֖י עַל־בֵּ֥ית
ג הָמָֽן: וַתּ֣וֹסֶף אֶסְתֵּ֗ר וַתְּדַבֵּר֙ לִפְנֵ֣י הַמֶּ֔לֶךְ
וַתִּפֹּ֖ל לִפְנֵ֣י רַגְלָ֑יו וַתֵּ֣בְךְּ וַתִּתְחַנֶּן־ל֗וֹ לְהַעֲבִיר֙ אֶת־רָעַת֙

that had happened to him, and his wise men and his wife, Zeresh, said to him, "If Mordechai, before whom you have begun to fall, is of Jewish descent, you will not prevail against him, but will undoubtedly fall before him." [14] While they were still talking with him, the king's chamberlains arrived, and they hurried to bring Haman to the banquet which Esther had prepared.

7 / 1. THE SECOND BANQUET: ESTHER PRESENTS HER REQUEST

It was one of God's miracles that, as disturbed as Ahasuerus was, he came to the feast, was cheered by the wine, and regained his good cheer to the extent that he was prepared to fulfill Esther's every wish.

3. The first הַמֶּלֶךְ, *King,* is taken to refer to God, the second to Ahasuerus. "Esther cast her eyes heavenward and said: 'If I have found favor in Your sight, O Supreme King, and if it pleases you, O King Ahasuerus, let my life be granted to me, and let my people be rescued out of the hands of the enemy' " (*Targum*).

6. HAMAN IS ACCUSED

7. The king went out to "cool off" from his anger, part of God's master plan, to give Haman the opportunity to incriminate himself even further in the king's absence.

9. HAMAN IS EXECUTED

Our Sages ordained that one should always say, חַרְבוֹנָה זָכוּר לַטוֹב — *"Harbonah of blessed memory,"* because it was Harbonah's swift advice that prevented Haman from possibly talking — or bribing — his way back into the king's good graces.

8 / 1. MORDECHAI IS APPOINTED PRIME MINISTER

3. ESTHER BEGS THE KING TO AVERT HAMAN'S DECREE

[1] So the king and Haman came to feast with Esther the queen. [2] The king asked Esther again on the second day at the wine feast, "What is your request, Esther the queen? — it shall be granted you. And what is your petition? [Even if it be] until half the kingdom, it shall be fulfilled." [3] So Esther the queen responded and said, "If I have found favor in your eyes, O king, and if it pleases the king, let my life be granted to me as my request and my people as my petition. [4] For we have been sold, I and my people, to be destroyed, to be slain and to be exterminated. Had we been sold as slaves and maidservants, I would have kept quiet, for the adversary is not worthy of the king's damage."

[5] Thereupon, King Ahasuerus exclaimed and said to Esther the queen, "Who is this? Where is this one who dared to do so?" [6] And Esther said, "A man who is an adversary and an enemy! This wicked Haman!" Haman trembled in terror before the king and queen. [7] The king rose in his wrath from the wine feast and went into the palace garden while Haman remained to beg Esther the queen for his soul, for he saw that evil had been determined against him by the king. [8] When the king returned from the palace garden to the hall of the wine feast, Haman had fallen onto the couch upon which Esther was; so the king exclaimed, "Would he actually assault the queen while I'm in the house?" As soon as the king uttered this, they covered Haman's face. [9] Then Harbonah, one of the chamberlains [in attendance] before the king, said, "Furthermore, the gallows which Haman made for Mordechai — who spoke good for the king — is standing in Haman's house; it is fifty cubits high." And the king said, "Hang him on it." [10] So they hanged Haman on the gallows that he had prepared for Mordechai, and the king's anger abated.

[1] That very day, King Ahasuerus gave the estate of Haman, the enemy of the Jews, to Esther the queen. Mordechai came before the king, for Esther had told [the king] what he was to her. [2] The king removed his signet ring, which he had taken away from Haman, and gave it to Mordechai; and Esther put Mordechai in charge of Haman's estate.

[3] Esther yet again spoke to the king, she fell at his feet, and wept and implored him to avert the evil [intention] of

הָמָן הָאֲגָגִי וְאֵת מַחֲשַׁבְתּוֹ אֲשֶׁר חָשַׁב עַל־הַיְּהוּדִים:

ד וַיּוֹשֶׁט הַמֶּלֶךְ לְאֶסְתֵּר אֵת שַׁרְבִט הַזָּהָב וַתָּקָם אֶסְתֵּר

ה וַתַּעֲמֹד לִפְנֵי הַמֶּלֶךְ: וַתֹּאמֶר אִם־עַל־הַמֶּלֶךְ טוֹב וְאִם־
מָצָאתִי חֵן לְפָנָיו וְכָשֵׁר הַדָּבָר לִפְנֵי הַמֶּלֶךְ וְטוֹבָה אֲנִי
בְּעֵינָיו יִכָּתֵב לְהָשִׁיב אֶת־הַסְּפָרִים מַחֲשֶׁבֶת הָמָן בֶּן־
הַמְּדָתָא הָאֲגָגִי אֲשֶׁר כָּתַב לְאַבֵּד אֶת־הַיְּהוּדִים אֲשֶׁר

ו בְּכָל־מְדִינוֹת הַמֶּלֶךְ: כִּי אֵיכָכָה אוּכַל וְרָאִיתִי בָּרָעָה
אֲשֶׁר־יִמְצָא אֶת־עַמִּי וְאֵיכָכָה אוּכַל וְרָאִיתִי בְּאָבְדַן

ז מוֹלַדְתִּי: וַיֹּאמֶר הַמֶּלֶךְ אֲחַשְׁוֵרֹשׁ לְאֶסְתֵּר
הַמַּלְכָּה וּלְמָרְדֳּכַי הַיְּהוּדִי הִנֵּה בֵית־הָמָן נָתַתִּי לְאֶסְתֵּר
וְאֹתוֹ תָּלוּ עַל־הָעֵץ עַל אֲשֶׁר־שָׁלַח יָדוֹ °בַּיְּהוּדִים

ח [°בִּיהוּדִיִּים כ׳] וְאַתֶּם כִּתְבוּ עַל־הַיְּהוּדִים כַּטּוֹב בְּעֵינֵיכֶם
בְּשֵׁם הַמֶּלֶךְ וְחִתְמוּ בְּטַבַּעַת הַמֶּלֶךְ כִּי־כְתָב אֲשֶׁר־נִכְתָּב
בְּשֵׁם־הַמֶּלֶךְ וְנַחְתּוֹם בְּטַבַּעַת הַמֶּלֶךְ אֵין לְהָשִׁיב: וַיִּקָּרְאוּ

ט סֹפְרֵי־הַמֶּלֶךְ בָּעֵת־הַהִיא בַּחֹדֶשׁ הַשְּׁלִישִׁי הוּא־חֹדֶשׁ סִיוָן
בִּשְׁלוֹשָׁה וְעֶשְׂרִים בּוֹ וַיִּכָּתֵב כְּכָל־אֲשֶׁר־צִוָּה מָרְדֳּכַי אֶל־
הַיְּהוּדִים וְאֶל הָאֲחַשְׁדַּרְפְּנִים וְהַפַּחוֹת וְשָׂרֵי הַמְּדִינוֹת
אֲשֶׁר מֵהֹדּוּ וְעַד־כּוּשׁ שֶׁבַע וְעֶשְׂרִים וּמֵאָה מְדִינָה מְדִינָה
וּמְדִינָה כִּכְתָבָהּ וְעַם וָעָם כִּלְשֹׁנוֹ וְאֶל־הַיְּהוּדִים כִּכְתָבָם

י וְכִלְשׁוֹנָם: וַיִּכְתֹּב בְּשֵׁם הַמֶּלֶךְ אֲחַשְׁוֵרֹשׁ וַיַּחְתֹּם בְּטַבַּעַת
הַמֶּלֶךְ וַיִּשְׁלַח סְפָרִים בְּיַד הָרָצִים בַּסּוּסִים רֹכְבֵי הָרֶכֶשׁ

יא הָאֲחַשְׁתְּרָנִים בְּנֵי הָרַמָּכִים: אֲשֶׁר נָתַן הַמֶּלֶךְ לַיְּהוּדִים ׀
אֲשֶׁר בְּכָל־עִיר־וָעִיר לְהִקָּהֵל וְלַעֲמֹד עַל־נַפְשָׁם לְהַשְׁמִיד
°וְלַהֲרֹג וּלְאַבֵּד אֶת־כָּל־חֵיל עַם וּמְדִינָה הַצָּרִים אֹתָם טַף

יב וְנָשִׁים וּשְׁלָלָם לָבוֹז: בְּיוֹם אֶחָד בְּכָל־מְדִינוֹת הַמֶּלֶךְ
אֲחַשְׁוֵרֹשׁ בִּשְׁלוֹשָׁה עָשָׂר לְחֹדֶשׁ שְׁנֵים־עָשָׂר הוּא־חֹדֶשׁ

יג אֲדָר: פַּתְשֶׁגֶן הַכְּתָב לְהִנָּתֵן דָּת בְּכָל־מְדִינָה וּמְדִינָה גָּלוּי
לְכָל־הָעַמִּים וְלִהְיוֹת °הַיְּהוּדִים עֲתִידִים [°הַיְּהוּדִיִּים כ׳]

יד עֲתוּדִים כ׳] לַיּוֹם הַזֶּה לְהִנָּקֵם מֵאֹיְבֵיהֶם: הָרָצִים רֹכְבֵי
הָרֶכֶשׁ הָאֲחַשְׁתְּרָנִים יָצְאוּ מְבֹהָלִים וּדְחוּפִים בִּדְבַר

טו הַמֶּלֶךְ וְהַדָּת נִתְּנָה בְּשׁוּשַׁן הַבִּירָה: **וּמָרְדֳּכַי**
יָצָא ׀ מִלִּפְנֵי הַמֶּלֶךְ בִּלְבוּשׁ מַלְכוּת תְּכֵלֶת וָחוּר
וַעֲטֶרֶת זָהָב גְּדוֹלָה וְתַכְרִיךְ בּוּץ וְאַרְגָּמָן וְהָעִיר שׁוּשָׁן

°נ״א לַהֲרֹג

Haman the Agagite, and his scheme that he had plotted against the Jews. [4] The king extended the gold scepter to Esther, and Esther arose and stood before the king. [5] She said, "If it pleases the king, and if I have found favor before him, and the proposal seems proper before the king, and I be pleasing in his eyes, let it be written to countermand those dispatches, the scheme of Haman the son of Hammedatha the Agagite, [in] which he had written to exterminate the Jews who are in all the king's provinces. [6] For how can I bear to witness the disaster which will befall my people?! How can I bear to witness the extermination of my kindred?!"

7. PERMISSION IS GRANTED TO OVERRIDE THE DECREE

[7] Then King Ahasuerus said to Esther the queen and to Mordechai the Jew, "Behold, I have given Haman's estate to Esther, and they have hanged him on the gallows because he sent [his] hand against the Jews. [8] You may write concerning the Jews whatever is favorable in your eyes, in the name of the king, and seal it with the king's signet, for an edict which is written in the king's name and sealed with the king's signet may not be revoked." [9] So they summoned the king's scribes at that time, in the third month, which is the month of Sivan, on its twenty-third [day], and it was written as Mordechai had dictated to the Jews and to the satraps, the governors and officials of the provinces from Hodu to Cush, a hundred and twenty-seven provinces, to each province in its own script, and each people in its own language, and to the Jews in their own script and language. [10] He wrote in the name of King Ahasuerus and sealed it with the king's signet. He sent dispatches by couriers on horseback, riders of swift mules bred of mares, [11] [to the effect] that the king had given [permission] to the Jews of every city to organize and to defend themselves; to destroy, to slay and to exterminate every armed force of any people or province that threaten them, [along with their] children and women, and to plunder their possessions, [12] on one day in all the provinces of King Ahasuerus, namely, upon the thirteenth day of the twelfth month, that is, the month of Adar. [13] Copies of the document were to be promulgated in every province, and be published to all peoples, for the Jews to be prepared for that day to avenge themselves on their enemies. [14] The couriers, riders of swift mules, went forth in urgent haste by word of the king, and the edict was distributed in Shushan the capital.

[15] **Mordechai left the king's presence clad in royal apparel of turquoise and white with a large gold crown and a robe of fine linen and purple; then the city of Shushan**

8. The Holy One, Blessed is He, now performed an unprecedented miracle. Was there ever in history such a miracle that Israel should wreak vengeance on the other nations and do with their enemies as they pleased? (*Midrash*).

11. Only by organizing and unifying themselves in begging for God's assistance could the Jews be victorious despite being seriously outnumbered.

15-16. These are among the four verses said aloud in the synagogue by the congregation during the public reading of the Megillah.

טז **צָהֲלָה וְשָׂמֵחָה: לַיְּהוּדִים הָיְתָה אוֹרָה וְשִׂמְחָה וְשָׂשֹׂן**
יז **וִיקָר:** וּבְכָל־מְדִינָה וּמְדִינָה וּבְכָל־עִיר וָעִיר מְקוֹם
אֲשֶׁר דְּבַר־הַמֶּלֶךְ וְדָתוֹ מַגִּיעַ שִׂמְחָה וְשָׂשׂוֹן לַיְּהוּדִים
מִשְׁתֶּה וְיוֹם טוֹב וְרַבִּים מֵעַמֵּי הָאָרֶץ מִתְיַהֲדִים כִּי־
ט א נָפַל פַּחַד־הַיְּהוּדִים עֲלֵיהֶם: וּבִשְׁנֵים עָשָׂר חֹדֶשׁ הוּא־
חֹדֶשׁ אֲדָר בִּשְׁלוֹשָׁה עָשָׂר יוֹם בּוֹ אֲשֶׁר הִגִּיעַ דְּבַר־
הַמֶּלֶךְ וְדָתוֹ לְהֵעָשׂוֹת בַּיּוֹם אֲשֶׁר שִׂבְּרוּ אֹיְבֵי הַיְּהוּדִים
לִשְׁלוֹט בָּהֶם וְנַהֲפוֹךְ הוּא אֲשֶׁר יִשְׁלְטוּ הַיְּהוּדִים
ב הֵמָּה בְּשֹׂנְאֵיהֶם: נִקְהֲלוּ הַיְּהוּדִים בְּעָרֵיהֶם בְּכָל־
מְדִינוֹת הַמֶּלֶךְ אֲחַשְׁוֵרוֹשׁ לִשְׁלֹחַ יָד בִּמְבַקְשֵׁי רָעָתָם
וְאִישׁ לֹא־עָמַד °לִפְנֵיהֶם כִּי־נָפַל פַּחְדָּם עַל־כָּל־ °נ״א בִּפְנֵיהֶם
ג הָעַמִּים: וְכָל־שָׂרֵי הַמְּדִינוֹת וְהָאֲחַשְׁדַּרְפְּנִים וְהַפַּחוֹת
וְעֹשֵׂי הַמְּלָאכָה אֲשֶׁר לַמֶּלֶךְ מְנַשְּׂאִים אֶת־הַיְּהוּדִים
ד כִּי־נָפַל פַּחַד־מָרְדֳּכַי עֲלֵיהֶם: כִּי־גָדוֹל מָרְדֳּכַי
בְּבֵית הַמֶּלֶךְ וְשָׁמְעוֹ הוֹלֵךְ בְּכָל־הַמְּדִינוֹת כִּי־הָאִישׁ
ה מָרְדֳּכַי הוֹלֵךְ וְגָדוֹל: וַיַּכּוּ הַיְּהוּדִים בְּכָל־אֹיְבֵיהֶם
מַכַּת־חֶרֶב וְהֶרֶג וְאַבְדָן וַיַּעֲשׂוּ בְשֹׂנְאֵיהֶם כִּרְצוֹנָם:
ו וּבְשׁוּשַׁן הַבִּירָה הָרְגוּ הַיְּהוּדִים וְאַבֵּד חֲמֵשׁ מֵאוֹת
ז אִישׁ: וְאֵת |
פַּרְשַׁנְדָּתָא וְאֵת |
דַּלְפוֹן וְאֵת |
ח אַסְפָּתָא: וְאֵת |
פּוֹרָתָא וְאֵת |
אֲדַלְיָא וְאֵת |
ט אֲרִידָתָא: וְאֵת |
פַּרְמַשְׁתָּא וְאֵת |
אֲרִיסַי וְאֵת |
אֲרִדַי וְאֵת |
י וַיְזָתָא:
עֲשֶׂרֶת
בְּנֵי הָמָן בֶּן־הַמְּדָתָא צֹרֵר הַיְּהוּדִים הָרָגוּ וּבַבִּזָּה לֹא
יא שָׁלְחוּ אֶת־יָדָם: בַּיּוֹם הַהוּא בָּא מִסְפַּר הַהֲרוּגִים בְּשׁוּשַׁן
יב הַבִּירָה לִפְנֵי הַמֶּלֶךְ: וַיֹּאמֶר הַמֶּלֶךְ לְאֶסְתֵּר הַמַּלְכָּה
בְּשׁוּשַׁן הַבִּירָה הָרְגוּ הַיְּהוּדִים וְאַבֵּד חֲמֵשׁ מֵאוֹת אִישׁ

16. "Rav Yehudah said אוֹרָה, *light,* refers to Torah; שְׂמְחָה, *gladness,* refers to holiday; שָׂשׂוֹן, *joy,* refers to circumcision; and יְקָר, *honor,* refers to תְּפִילִין, *tefillin* [i.e., they were finally able to resume the study of Torah and without hindrance] the performance of *mitzvos*" (*Talmud*).

9 / 1. THE TURNABOUT: THE JEWS AVENGE THEMSELVES

7. The 10 sons of Haman and the word עֲשֶׂרֶת, *10,* which follows, should be said [by one reading the Megillah on Purim] in one breath ... to indicate that they all died together (*Talmud*).

9. The letter *vav* [ו] of *Vayzasa* is enlarged in the Megillah like a long pole to indicate that they were all strung [one underneath the other] to one long pole (*Talmud*).

10. It was obviously most difficult for poor Jews to restrain themselves from taking spoils. In reward for their restraint, it was established that, throughout all generations, the poor — without exception and investigation as to need — will be the recipients of מַתָּנוֹת לָאֶבְיוֹנִים, *gifts to the poor* (*Rebbe of Ger*).

was cheerful and glad. [16] **The Jews had light and gladness and joy and honor.** [17] And in every province, and in every city, every place where the king's word and his decree reached, the Jews had gladness and joy, a feast and a holiday. Moreover, many from among the people of the land professed themselves Jews, for the fear of the Jews had fallen upon them.

[1] Then, in the twelfth month, which is the month of Adar, on its thirteenth day, when the king's command and edict were about to be enforced, on the day that the enemies of the Jews expected to prevail over them, and it was turned about: The Jews prevailed over their adversaries. [2] The Jews organized themselves in their cities in all the provinces of King Ahasuerus, to send forth [their] hand against those who sought their hurt; and no man could stand before them, for fear of them had fallen upon all the peoples. [3] And all the officials of the provinces, the satraps and the governors and those that conduct the king's affairs, exalted the Jews for the fear of Mordechai had fallen upon them. [4] For Mordechai was now pre-eminent in the royal palace and his fame was spreading throughout all the provinces, for the man Mordechai grew increasingly greater. [5] And the Jews struck at all their enemies with the stroke of the sword, slaughtering and annihilating; they treated their enemies as they pleased. [6] In Shushan the capital, the Jews slew and annihilated five hundred men.

[7] and Parshandatha and Dalphon and Aspatha [8] and Poratha and Adalia and Aridatha [9] and Parmashta and Arisai and Aridai and Vaizatha [10] the ten sons of Haman son of Hammedatha, the Jews' enemy; but they did not lay their hand on the spoils.

[11] That same day the number of those killed in Shushan the capital was reported to the king. [12] The king said to Esther the queen, "In Shushan the capital the Jews have slain and annihilated five hundred men, as well as

וְאֵת עֲשֶׂרֶת בְּנֵי־הָמָן בִּשְׁאָר מְדִינוֹת הַמֶּלֶךְ מֶה עָשׂוּ וּמַה־

יג שְׁאֵלָתֵךְ וְיִנָּתֵן לָךְ וּמַה־בַּקָּשָׁתֵךְ עוֹד וְתֵעָשׂ: וַתֹּאמֶר אֶסְתֵּר
אִם־עַל־הַמֶּלֶךְ טוֹב יִנָּתֵן גַּם־מָחָר לַיְּהוּדִים אֲשֶׁר בְּשׁוּשָׁן
לַעֲשׂוֹת כְּדָת הַיּוֹם וְאֵת עֲשֶׂרֶת בְּנֵי־הָמָן יִתְלוּ עַל־הָעֵץ:

יד וַיֹּאמֶר הַמֶּלֶךְ לְהֵעָשׂוֹת כֵּן וַתִּנָּתֵן דָּת בְּשׁוּשָׁן וְאֵת עֲשֶׂרֶת
בְּנֵי־הָמָן תָּלוּ: וַיִּקָּהֲלוּ °הַיְּהוּדִים [°הַיְּהוּדִיים כ] אֲשֶׁר־

טו בְּשׁוּשָׁן גַּם בְּיוֹם אַרְבָּעָה עָשָׂר לְחֹדֶשׁ אֲדָר וַיַּהַרְגוּ
בְשׁוּשָׁן שְׁלֹשׁ מֵאוֹת אִישׁ וּבַבִּזָּה לֹא שָׁלְחוּ אֶת־יָדָם:

טז וּשְׁאָר הַיְּהוּדִים אֲשֶׁר בִּמְדִינוֹת הַמֶּלֶךְ נִקְהֲלוּ ׀ וְעָמֹד עַל־
נַפְשָׁם וְנוֹחַ מֵאֹיְבֵיהֶם וְהָרוֹג בְּשֹׂנְאֵיהֶם חֲמִשָּׁה וְשִׁבְעִים

יז אֶלֶף וּבַבִּזָּה לֹא שָׁלְחוּ אֶת־יָדָם: בְּיוֹם־שְׁלֹשָׁה עָשָׂר
לְחֹדֶשׁ אֲדָר וְנוֹחַ בְּאַרְבָּעָה עָשָׂר בּוֹ וְעָשֹׂה אֹתוֹ יוֹם

יח מִשְׁתֶּה וְשִׂמְחָה: °וְהַיְּהוּדִים [°וְהַיְּהוּדִיים כ] אֲשֶׁר־בְּשׁוּשָׁן
נִקְהֲלוּ בִּשְׁלֹשָׁה עָשָׂר בּוֹ וּבְאַרְבָּעָה עָשָׂר בּוֹ וְנוֹחַ בַּחֲמִשָּׁה

יט עָשָׂר בּוֹ וְעָשֹׂה אֹתוֹ יוֹם מִשְׁתֶּה וְשִׂמְחָה: עַל־כֵּן
הַיְּהוּדִים °הַפְּרָזִים [°הַפְּרוֹזִים כ] הַיֹּשְׁבִים בְּעָרֵי הַפְּרָזוֹת
עֹשִׂים אֵת יוֹם אַרְבָּעָה עָשָׂר לְחֹדֶשׁ אֲדָר שִׂמְחָה וּמִשְׁתֶּה

כ וְיוֹם טוֹב וּמִשְׁלוֹחַ מָנוֹת אִישׁ לְרֵעֵהוּ: וַיִּכְתֹּב מָרְדֳּכַי אֶת־
הַדְּבָרִים הָאֵלֶּה וַיִּשְׁלַח סְפָרִים אֶל־כָּל־הַיְּהוּדִים אֲשֶׁר
בְּכָל־מְדִינוֹת הַמֶּלֶךְ אֲחַשְׁוֵרוֹשׁ הַקְּרוֹבִים וְהָרְחוֹקִים:

כא לְקַיֵּם עֲלֵיהֶם לִהְיוֹת עֹשִׂים אֵת יוֹם אַרְבָּעָה עָשָׂר לְחֹדֶשׁ

כב אֲדָר וְאֵת יוֹם־חֲמִשָּׁה עָשָׂר בּוֹ בְּכָל־שָׁנָה וְשָׁנָה: כַּיָּמִים
אֲשֶׁר־נָחוּ בָהֶם הַיְּהוּדִים מֵאֹיְבֵיהֶם וְהַחֹדֶשׁ אֲשֶׁר נֶהְפַּךְ
לָהֶם מִיָּגוֹן לְשִׂמְחָה וּמֵאֵבֶל לְיוֹם טוֹב לַעֲשׂוֹת אוֹתָם יְמֵי
מִשְׁתֶּה וְשִׂמְחָה וּמִשְׁלֹחַ מָנוֹת אִישׁ לְרֵעֵהוּ וּמַתָּנוֹת

כג לָאֶבְיוֹנִים: וְקִבֵּל הַיְּהוּדִים אֵת אֲשֶׁר־הֵחֵלּוּ לַעֲשׂוֹת וְאֵת

כד אֲשֶׁר־כָּתַב מָרְדֳּכַי אֲלֵיהֶם: כִּי הָמָן בֶּן־הַמְּדָתָא הָאֲגָגִי
צֹרֵר כָּל־הַיְּהוּדִים חָשַׁב עַל־הַיְּהוּדִים לְאַבְּדָם וְהִפִּל פּוּר

כה הוּא הַגּוֹרָל לְהֻמָּם וּלְאַבְּדָם: וּבְבֹאָהּ לִפְנֵי הַמֶּלֶךְ אָמַר
עִם־הַסֵּפֶר יָשׁוּב מַחֲשַׁבְתּוֹ הָרָעָה אֲשֶׁר־חָשַׁב עַל־

כו הַיְּהוּדִים עַל־רֹאשׁוֹ וְתָלוּ אֹתוֹ וְאֶת־בָּנָיו עַל־הָעֵץ: עַל־
כֵּן קָרְאוּ לַיָּמִים הָאֵלֶּה פוּרִים עַל־שֵׁם הַפּוּר עַל־כֵּן עַל־
כָּל־דִּבְרֵי הָאִגֶּרֶת הַזֹּאת וּמָה־רָאוּ עַל־כָּכָה וּמָה הִגִּיעַ

the ten sons of Haman; what have they done in the rest of the king's provinces?! What is your request now? It shall be granted you. What is your petition further? It shall be fulfilled.'' [13] Esther replied, ''If it pleases the king, let tomorrow also be given to the Jews who are in Shushan to act as they did today, and let Haman's ten sons be hanged on the gallows.'' [14] The king ordered that this be done, and a decree was distributed in Shushan; and they hanged Haman's ten sons. [15] The Jews that were in Shushan assembled again on the fourteenth day of the month of Adar and slew three hundred men in Shushan; but they did not lay their hand on the spoils.

[16] The rest of the Jews that were in the king's provinces assembled and defended themselves gaining relief from their foes, slaying seventy-five thousand of their enemies, but they did not lay their hand on the spoils, [17] on the thirteenth day of the month of Adar. And they gained relief on its fourteenth [day], making it a day of feasting and gladness. [18] But the Jews that were in Shushan assembled on both its thirteenth [day] and its fourteenth, and they gained relief on its fifteenth, making it a day of feasting and gladness. [19] Therefore, Jewish villagers who live in unwalled towns celebrate the fourteenth day of the month of Adar as an occasion of gladness, feasting and festival, and for sending delicacies to one another.

[20] Mordechai recorded these events and sent letters to all the Jews who were in all the provinces of King Ahasuerus, the near ones and the distant ones, [21] [charging them] to observe annually the fourteenth day of the month of Adar and its fifteenth day, [22] as the days on which the Jews gained relief from their enemies, and the month which had been turned about for them from one of sorrow to gladness, and from mourning to festival; to observe them as days of feasting and gladness, and sending delicacies to each other, and gifts to the poor. [23] The Jews undertook [to continue] that which they had begun, just as Mordechai had prescribed to them.

[24] For Haman son Hammedatha the Agagite, enemy of all the Jews, had plotted to annihilate the Jews and had cast a pur (that is, the lot) to terrify and to annihilate them. [25] But when she appeared before the king, he commanded by means of letters that [Haman's] wicked scheme, which he had devised against the Jews, should recoil on his own head; and they hanged him and his sons on the gallows. [26] Therefore, they called these days ''Purim'' from the word ''pur.'' Therefore, because of all that was written in this letter, and because of what they had seen concerning this, and what has happened to them,

19. The law of "Shushan Purim" — celebrating Purim on the 15th day of Adar in walled cities in commemoration of the victory in Shushan — is not specifically stated in the Megillah. It is implied in verses 19 and 21 and so established by the Rabbis.

20. MORDECHAI RECORDS THESE EVENTS AND LEGISLATES ANNUAL COMMEMORATION
He wrote this Megillah exactly as it appears in its present text.

22. *Sending delicacies to each other* — at least two *delicacies*, i.e., ready-to-eat foods [מָנוֹת being plural] to one man. *And gifts to the poor* — this means two gifts to two men [one gift to each of the two, the minimum number of the plural אֶבְיוֹנִים, *poor*, being two] (*Talmud*).

אֲלֵיהֶם: קִיְּמוּ °וְקִבְּלוּ [°וְקִבֵּל כ·] הַיְּהוּדִים`| עֲלֵיהֶם`| וְעַל־
זַרְעָם וְעַל כָּל־הַנִּלְוִים עֲלֵיהֶם וְלֹא יַעֲבוֹר לִהְיוֹת עֹשִׂים
אֵת־שְׁנֵי הַיָּמִים הָאֵלֶּה כִּכְתָבָם וְכִזְמַנָּם בְּכָל־שָׁנָה וְשָׁנָה:
וְהַיָּמִים הָאֵלֶּה נִזְכָּרִים וְנַעֲשִׂים בְּכָל־דּוֹר וָדוֹר מִשְׁפָּחָה
וּמִשְׁפָּחָה מְדִינָה וּמְדִינָה וְעִיר וָעִיר וִימֵי הַפּוּרִים הָאֵלֶּה
לֹא יַעַבְרוּ מִתּוֹךְ הַיְּהוּדִים וְזִכְרָם לֹא־יָסוּף מִזַּרְעָם:
וַתִּכְתֹּב אֶסְתֵּר הַמַּלְכָּה בַת־אֲבִיחַיִל וּמָרְדֳּכַי הַיְּהוּדִי
אֶת־כָּל־תֹּקֶף לְקַיֵּם אֵת אִגֶּרֶת הַפֻּרִים הַזֹּאת הַשֵּׁנִית:
וַיִּשְׁלַח סְפָרִים אֶל־כָּל־הַיְּהוּדִים אֶל־שֶׁבַע וְעֶשְׂרִים וּמֵאָה
מְדִינָה מַלְכוּת אֲחַשְׁוֵרוֹשׁ דִּבְרֵי שָׁלוֹם וֶאֱמֶת: לְקַיֵּם אֶת־
יְמֵי הַפֻּרִים הָאֵלֶּה בִּזְמַנֵּיהֶם כַּאֲשֶׁר קִיַּם עֲלֵיהֶם מָרְדֳּכַי
הַיְּהוּדִי וְאֶסְתֵּר הַמַּלְכָּה וְכַאֲשֶׁר קִיְּמוּ עַל־נַפְשָׁם וְעַל־
זַרְעָם דִּבְרֵי הַצּוֹמוֹת וְזַעֲקָתָם: וּמַאֲמַר אֶסְתֵּר קִיַּם דִּבְרֵי
הַפֻּרִים הָאֵלֶּה וְנִכְתָּב בַּסֵּפֶר: וַיָּשֶׂם הַמֶּלֶךְ
°אֲחַשְׁוֵרוֹשׁ [°אֲחַשְׁרֹשׁ כ·] | מַס עַל־הָאָרֶץ וְאִיֵּי הַיָּם:
וְכָל־מַעֲשֵׂה תָקְפּוֹ וּגְבוּרָתוֹ וּפָרָשַׁת גְּדֻלַּת מָרְדֳּכַי אֲשֶׁר
גִּדְּלוֹ הַמֶּלֶךְ הֲלוֹא־הֵם כְּתוּבִים עַל־סֵפֶר דִּבְרֵי הַיָּמִים
לְמַלְכֵי מָדַי וּפָרָס: **כִּי | מָרְדֳּכַי הַיְּהוּדִי מִשְׁנֶה לַמֶּלֶךְ
אֲחַשְׁוֵרוֹשׁ וְגָדוֹל לַיְּהוּדִים וְרָצוּי לְרֹב אֶחָיו דֹּרֵשׁ טוֹב
לְעַמּוֹ וְדֹבֵר שָׁלוֹם לְכָל־זַרְעוֹ:**

After the reading of the Megillah, say:

בָּרוּךְ אַתָּה יהוה אֱלֹהֵינוּ מֶלֶךְ הָעוֹלָם, (הָאֵל) הָרָב אֶת
רִיבֵנוּ, וְהַדָּן אֶת דִּינֵנוּ, וְהַנּוֹקֵם אֶת נִקְמָתֵנוּ, וְהַמְשַׁלֵּם
גְּמוּל לְכָל אֹיְבֵי נַפְשֵׁנוּ, וְהַנִּפְרָע לָנוּ מִצָּרֵינוּ. בָּרוּךְ
אַתָּה יהוה, הַנִּפְרָע לְעַמּוֹ יִשְׂרָאֵל מִכָּל צָרֵיהֶם, הָאֵל
הַמּוֹשִׁיעַ.

27. *Confirmed and undertook —* i.e., they confirmed what they had undertaken long before at Sinai (*Talmud*).

28. "Even if all the festivals should be annulled, Purim will never be annulled" (*Midrash*).

29. וַתִּכְתֹּב — *Wrote.* The letter ת in this word is enlarged to indicate that just as the ת is the last letter of the alphabet, so is the story of Esther the end of all the miracles to be included in the Torah (*Talmud*).

[27] the Jews confirmed and undertook upon themselves, and their posterity, and upon all who might join them, without fail, to observe these two days, in their prescribed manner, and in their proper time each year. [28] And these days should be remembered and celebrated by every generation, every family, every province, and every city; and these days of Purim should never cease among the Jews, nor shall their remembrance perish from their descendants.

[29] Then Esther the queen daughter of Abihail wrote, along with Mordechai the Jew, with full authority to ratify this second letter of Purim. [30] Dispatches were sent to all the Jews, to the hundred and twenty-seven provinces of the kingdom of Ahasuerus — [with] words of peace and truth — [31] to establish these days of Purim on their [proper] dates just as Mordechai the Jew and Esther the queen had enjoined them, and as they had confirmed upon themselves and their posterity the matter of the fasts and their lamentations. [32] Esther's ordinance confirmed these regulations for Purim; and it was recorded in the book.

10 / I. EPILOGUE

With the salvation of the Jews, affairs of state returned to normal. Under Mordechai, the empire grew stronger.

3. With the mention of שָׁלוֹם, *welfare* [literally, *peace*], and a picture of the stature and security of the Jews under Mordechai, the Megillah closes.

The last verse of the Megillah is among the four verses read aloud by the congregation during the reading of the Megillah in the synagogue. Among the reasons offered for this widespread custom are: to popularize the miracle [פִּירְסוּמֵי נִיסָא]; these verses express the essence of the miracle through Mordechai; and to keep the children alert and prevent them from dozing off. The congregation recites the verses loudly as an expression of the joy of the day. The reader then repeats the verses because each verse must be read from the Megillah.

[1] King Ahasuerus levied a tax on the mainland and the islands of the sea. [2] All his mighty and powerful acts, and the account of the greatness of Mordechai, whom the king had promoted, are recorded in the book of chronicles of the kings of Media and Persia. [3] **For Mordechai the Jew was viceroy to King Ahasuerus; he was a great man among the Jews, and found favor with the multitude of his brethren; he sought the good of his people and spoke for the welfare of all his seed.**

After the reading of the Megillah, say:

Blessed are You, Hᴀsʜᴇᴍ, our God, King of the universe, (the God) Who takes up our grievance, judges our claim, avenges our wrong; Who brings just retribution upon all enemies of our soul and exacts vengeance for us from our foes. Blessed are You, Hᴀsʜᴇᴍ, Who exacts vengeance for His people Israel from all their foes, the God Who brings salvation.

After the nighttime Megillah reading, the following two paragraphs are recited.
After the daytime reading, continue with שׁוֹשַׁנַּת יַעֲקֹב below.

אֲשֶׁר הֵנִיא עֲצַת גּוֹיִם, וַיָּפֶר מַחְשְׁבוֹת עֲרוּמִים.

בְּקוּם עָלֵינוּ אָדָם רָשָׁע, נֵצֶר זָדוֹן, מִזֶּרַע עֲמָלֵק.

גָּאָה בְעָשְׁרוֹ, וְכָרָה לוֹ בּוֹר, וּגְדֻלָּתוֹ יָקְשָׁה לּוֹ לָכֶד.

דִּמָּה בְנַפְשׁוֹ לִלְכּוֹד, וְנִלְכַּד, בִּקֵּשׁ לְהַשְׁמִיד, וְנִשְׁמַד מְהֵרָה.

הָמָן הוֹדִיעַ אֵיבַת אֲבוֹתָיו, וְעוֹרֵר שִׂנְאַת אַחִים לַבָּנִים.

וְלֹא זָכַר רַחֲמֵי שָׁאוּל, כִּי בְחֶמְלָתוֹ עַל אֲגָג נוֹלַד אוֹיֵב.

זָמַם רָשָׁע לְהַכְרִית צַדִּיק, וְנִלְכַּד טָמֵא בִּידֵי טָהוֹר.

חֶסֶד גָּבַר עַל שִׁגְגַת אָב, וְרָשָׁע הוֹסִיף חֵטְא עַל חֲטָאָיו.

טָמַן בְּלִבּוֹ מַחְשְׁבוֹת עֲרוּמָיו, וַיִּתְמַכֵּר לַעֲשׂוֹת רָעָה.

יָדוֹ שָׁלַח בִּקְדוֹשֵׁי אֵל, כַּסְפּוֹ נָתַן לְהַכְרִית זִכְרָם.

בִּרְאוֹת מָרְדְּכַי, כִּי יָצָא קֶצֶף, וְדָתֵי הָמָן נִתְּנוּ בְשׁוּשָׁן.

לָבַשׁ שַׂק וְקָשַׁר מִסְפֵּד, וְגָזַר צוֹם וַיֵּשֶׁב עַל הָאֵפֶר.

מִי זֶה יַעֲמֹד לְכַפֵּר שְׁגָגָה, וְלִמְחֹל חַטַּאת עֲוֺן אֲבוֹתֵינוּ.

נֵץ פָּרַח מִלּוּלָב, הֵן הֲדַסָּה עָמְדָה לְעוֹרֵר יְשֵׁנִים.

סָרִיסֶיהָ הִבְהִילוּ לְהָמָן, לְהַשְׁקוֹתוֹ יֵין חֲמַת תַּנִּינִים.

עָמַד בְּעָשְׁרוֹ, וְנָפַל בְּרִשְׁעוֹ, עָשָׂה לוֹ עֵץ, וְנִתְלָה עָלָיו.

פִּיהֶם פָּתְחוּ כָּל יוֹשְׁבֵי תֵבֵל, כִּי פוּר הָמָן נֶהְפַּךְ לְפוּרֵנוּ.

צַדִּיק נֶחֱלַץ מִיַּד רָשָׁע, אוֹיֵב נִתַּן תַּחַת נַפְשׁוֹ.

קִיְּמוּ עֲלֵיהֶם, לַעֲשׂוֹת פּוּרִים, וְלִשְׂמֹחַ בְּכָל שָׁנָה וְשָׁנָה.

רָאִיתָ אֶת תְּפִלַּת מָרְדְּכַי וְאֶסְתֵּר, הָמָן וּבָנָיו עַל הָעֵץ תָּלִיתָ.

The following is recited after both Megillah readings.

שׁוֹשַׁנַּת יַעֲקֹב צָהֲלָה וְשָׂמֵחָה,
בִּרְאוֹתָם יַחַד תְּכֵלֶת מָרְדְּכָי.

תְּשׁוּעָתָם הָיִיתָ לָנֶצַח, וְתִקְוָתָם בְּכָל דּוֹר וָדוֹר.

לְהוֹדִיעַ, שֶׁכָּל קֹוֶיךָ לֹא יֵבֹשׁוּ,

וְלֹא יִכָּלְמוּ לָנֶצַח כָּל הַחוֹסִים בָּךְ.

אָרוּר הָמָן, אֲשֶׁר בִּקֵּשׁ לְאַבְּדִי, בָּרוּךְ מָרְדְּכַי הַיְּהוּדִי.

אֲרוּרָה זֶרֶשׁ, אֵשֶׁת מַפְחִידִי, בְּרוּכָה אֶסְתֵּר בַּעֲדִי,

וְגַם חַרְבוֹנָה זָכוּר לַטּוֹב.